Mind the Lin
Golf Memories

BILLY DETTLAFF
PAUL S PHILIPPOU
JIM MACKINTOSH
LORRAINE YOUNG

TIPPERMUIR
BOOKS LIMITED

Car park at The Open, Carnoustie, 1953

Mind the Links: Golf Memories – Billy Dettlaff, Paul S Philippou,
Jim Mackintosh & Lorraine Young

Copyright © 2022. All rights reserved.

Kingarrock Hickory Golf by Dan Barlow is copyright National Trust for Scotland.

The right of the contributors to the book (as listed therein) to be identified
as the authors of the Work has been asserted in accordance with
the Copyright, Designs & Patents Act 1988.

This first edition published and copyright 2022 by
Tippermuir Books Ltd, Perth, Scotland.

mail@tippermuirbooks.co.uk – www.tippermuirbooks.co.uk

No part of this publication may be reproduced or used in any form
or by any means without written permission from the Publisher
except for review purposes.

All rights whatsoever in this book are reserved.

ISBN 978-1-913836-19-1 (paperback).

A CIP catalogue record for this book is available from the British Library.

Copyright of DC Thomson, Donald Ford and Getty Images photographs
are acknowledged.

Project coordination by Dr Paul S Philippou.

Cover design by Matthew Mackie.

Editorial support: Steve Zajda and Jean Hands.

Text design, layout, and artwork by Bernard Chandler [graffik].
Text set in Gill Sans Std Light 13/17pt with Gill Sans Std Regular titling.

Printed and bound by Ashford Colour Press, Gosport, Hampshire PO13 0FW

Acknowledgements

Golf Memories wishes to record their deepest gratitude to Billy Dettlaff, for his generous support of this book but above all his belief in what we do. Without his drive, encouragement and assistance we would still be at the 1st tee hoping to get a game.

Golf Memories also owes a debt of gratitude to Jim Mackintosh, editor of *Mind the Time*, who was the initiator of the idea to produce *Mind the Links: Golf Memories*, which has been published in honour of the 150th Open taking place at St Andrews in July 2022. His love for the game has shone throughout this journey and is reflected in the poetic works produced.

Thanks go to Dr Paul S Philippou who has guided us through the whole production process with diplomacy and calm but with great enthusiasm to ensure that the product reflects the sheer joy we experience every day in the company of our members. And to the team at Tippermuir: Bernard Chandler for his graphic work, Steve Zajda and Jean Hands for their proof-reading and Matthew Mackie for the book cover.

The support from the following people has been appreciated:
All the volunteers at Golf Memories who so tirelessly give of their time to help us unlock and retrieve an amazing wealth of golden memories. They are the backbone and life blood behind all we do.

All our friends from the USA and those associated in any way with The Pete Dye Chapter.

Kevin Barker – The R&A

Graham Barr – Scottish Golf

Steve Finan – *Author of Golf In Scotland In The Black & White Era* (2022)

Hannah Fleming and Angela Howe – The R&A World Golf Museum

John Gilbert – Captain Carnoustie Golf Club

Richard McBrearty – Memories Scotland

Michael Wells – CE Carnoustie Golf Links

And all those who have contributed to the book in any form.

Thanks go to the following for allowing us permission to use photographs from their archives and to all those who provided photographs for the book.

Every attempt has been made to acknowledge those who have given permission for their photographs to be used. If we have omitted anyone, please accept our sincere apologies:

David Cannon

Getty Images

The R&A

The R&A World Golf Museum

D C Thomson

Golf Memories is entirely volunteer led and run. Its funding comes through donations and fund raising. It is supported by the following organisations:

Carnoustie Golf Links

Scottish Golf

The R&A

The R&A World Golf Museum

OTHER POETRY TITLES BY TIPPERMUIR BOOKS

Walking with Ghosts *(Alan Laing, 2017)*

Flipstones *(Jim Mackintosh, 2018)*

A Little Book of Carol's *(Carol Page, 2018)*

A Squatter o Bairnrhymes *(Stuart Paterson, 2020)*

The Nicht Afore Christmas *(Irene McFarlane and Rosemary Cunningham, 2020)*

In a Sma Room Songbook: From the Poems by William Soutar *(Debra Salem (ed), 2020)*

Beyond the Swelkie *(Jim Mackintosh and Paul S Philippou (eds), 2021)*

FORTHCOMING

William Soutar: Collected Poetry, Volume I (Published Work)
(Kirsteen McCue, Philippa Osmond-Williams and Paul S Philippou (eds), 2022)

William Soutar: Collected Poetry, Volume II (Published Work)
(Kirsteen McCue, Philippa Osmond-Williams and Paul S Philippou (eds), 2022)

William Soutar: Collected Poetry, Volume III (Unublished Work)
(Kirsteen McCue, Philippa Osmond-Williams and Paul S Philippou (eds), 2023)

Perthshire 101 *(Andy Jackson (ed), 2022)*

Berries Fae Banes: An Owersettin in Scots o the Poems bi Pino Mereu scrievit in Tribute tae Hamish Henderson
(Jim Mackintosh, 2022)

Contents

Foreword – Lorraine Young... 1
Preface – Billy Dettlaff... 5
Mind the Links – Michael Wells.. 13
Words of an Open Champion – Paul Lawrie 18
The Barry – Jim Mackintosh... 22
Scottish Golf – Graham Barr 24
Michael Ego's Golf and Sports Remembrances – Kimi Ego .. 27
Captain of the Royal & Ancient Golf Club of St Andrews –
    George McGregor.. 30
The Swilcan – William Caine.. 36
On The Road – Paul Forsyth... 37
But the Sea is – Larissa Reid 43
Walking with Sandy, Seve and Dad – Peter Roy 45
My Golfing Life – Patricia Sawers 47
The Caddy – Jennie Turnbull... 51
Some Memories – Trevor Williamson................................ 53
A Round on the 'Big' Course & Pic of the Day –
    Donald Ford 64
Carnoustie Links – Patrick Healy 69
A Memory – Michael Breed... 70
The Arnie Piece – Jim Nugent... 73
Blairgowrie – Ann MacLaren... 75
Henry – Jim Mackintosh... 77

Memories of Musselburgh – *Mungo Park* 79

Musselburgh 1566 – *Finola Scott* 83

A Link with Peter and Alice Dye – *Billy Dettlaff* 84

Extracts from Dreams of Scottish Youth – *Graham Fulton* ... 88

The Victory – *Ross Kilvington* 90

The Gowf Experience – *Sheila Templeton* 94

Tiger – *Hugh MacDonald* 96

It's a Breeze – *Roy Mackenzie* 102

When the Chips are Down – *Diane McKee* 103

Gift – *Yvonne Gray* 105

Shanks for the Good Times – *Steve Finan* 108

Quaint Customs and No Pints for Ladies – *Rona Fitzgerald* 112

A Song of Putting – *W M Lindsay* 114

Golf in a Scottish Winter – *Colin MacLean* 116

Kingarrock Hickory Golf – *Dan Barlow* 119

A Set of Swilken of St Andrews 'QE2' Limited Edition Clubs–
  Lindsay Ewart 123

Arbroath Artisans – *Lynn Valentine* 124

Recollections from an Arbroath Artisan Member –
  Bernie Mortimer 125

That's Golf! – *Susan Grant* 127

Royal Dornoch – *Gordon Bannerman* 129

Missing The Cut – *Andy Jackson* 134

In the Bunker – *Julie McNeill* 136

Pete's Greatest Legacy – *Bobby Weed* 139

Golf Island – *W N Herbert*... 143

Amen – *Graham Fulton*.. 145

The Youngest Champion–Memories of Nancy Jupp –
  Peter Lowe.. 148

I Think of the Woman Who Dives for Golf Balls –
  Yvonne Gray 157

A Fox in the Hen House! – *Louise Graham* 158

I Don't Remember Nicklaus – *Keith McIntosh*............. 160

Willie's Golf Story… – *Lorraine Young*........................ 162

Gary Player at Carnoustie – *John Quinn* 169

Some Thoughts on Some Stories from Yesteryear –
  Lee Vannet.. 170

My Golfing Pal – *Olive M Ritch*................................... 178

Murdo – *Leela Soma*... 180

The Man I Called Nana – *Charles D Burgess* 182

Where Have all the Golf Balls Gone? Long Time Passing –
  Euan Kerr 188

Formative Years at Carnoustie – *David Blair* 191

Elegy for Peter Alliss – *Andy Jackson* 194

Bow Before the King of the Windmills – *Stephen Watt*... 195

How to Punch – *Victoria McNulty* 197

Golf in my Veins – *A Carnoustian*............................... 198

1984 – *Graham Fulton* 204

Golf For All – *Andrew Murray*..................................... 208

My Golf Memories – *Leslie (Les) Schupak*................... 209

The 16th, Old Tom's Pulpit – *Morag Anderson* 212

Stornoway Golf Course – *Donald Murray* 213

What do you Collect? – *James Davis* 214

In The Swing – *Aileen Ballantyne (neé Guthrie)* 216

A Golfer's Tale – *George Constable* 218

Up Glencruitten Golf Course – *Andy Breckenridge* 219

Crazy Happy – Crazy Golf – *Gabrielle Barnby* 221

Stunting – *Graham Fulton* 223

On The Road – *Debbie Foley* 225

A Poem from Coronaworld, May 2020 – *Graham Fulton* 228

Carnoustie Craws Junior Golf Academy –
Poetry Competition Entries 231

The Fifth Major in Golf – *Michael White* 236

Cherishing Memories – *Richard McBrearty* 240

R&A World Golf Museum – *Hannah Fleming* 243

Golf Memories 245

Golf Memories: Member, Carer and Family
    Commendations 247

Golf Memories Cards 248

Series of Images of Golf Memory Cards 249

Links Song – *W G Strachan* 276

About The Contributors – *The Aficionados of Golf* 277

Other Titles by Tippermuir Books 290

**The Queen's Award
for Voluntary Service**

Carnoustie Memories 2022

'Every day, millions of people across the UK are making a difference by volunteering. Each year, outstanding examples of this work are celebrated through the Queen's Award for Voluntary Service (QAVS). Created in 2002 for the Queen's Golden Jubilee, QAVS awards have been shining a light on the fantastic work of voluntary groups for many years. Equivalent to an MBE, QAVS are the highest awards given to local voluntary groups in the UK, and they are awarded for life.'

Golf Memories, 147th Open, Carnoustie 2018

Foreword

LORRAINE YOUNG

Mind the Links: Golf Memories is intended as a trigger for individuals to recall their 'Golf Memories' and personal memorable moments. The images within the book will stimulate rich conversations.

What an amazing journey Golf Memories has been and accompanied by the nicest group of people one could ever imagine. My retirement wish was to be able to give something back to our community which would be free to all and specifically to bridge the gap between established public services and voluntary work with those living with dementia.

Our journey as a group, 100 per cent volunteer led and managed, started back in 2014 when planning for the establishment of Golf Memories Carnoustie commenced followed swiftly by the launch in 2015. I was thrilled that everything fell into place so quickly, but I had no true idea as to the shape our journey would go on to take.

The importance of cherishing memories whilst creating new memories was one thing, but the sheer range and diversity of the memories that flowed was and still is breathtaking and created the ever-present question as to how to capture these magical moments.

Witnessing first-hand the transformation that came over our members when they spent time together, recalling their magical moments in golf using a range of memorabilia and memory cards was I thought the best feeling in the world. But then add the dimension of physical activity and you must be prepared to be 'blown away', as a friend, the late Professor Michael Ego from Connecticut University, described how he felt after visiting and witnessing our group in action.

The simple act of holding a golf club once again is transformational to watch as the individual adjusts their grip on the club and prepares their stance in the address position. Rewind to a gentleman arriving in a wheelchair and placed by the carer beside a life-size image of his hero Gary Player, sitting with his head bowed, showing little interest in anything around him to the same gent leaving the group sometime later having sunk a putt out on the putting green. He stood there with the broadest of smiles and gave a 'thumbs up' whilst announcing to the world 'GREAT!' The impact of the recognisable smell of the freshly mown grass; the sea breeze on his face and the inherent lure of competition and camaraderie all came flowing back. What is there not to love about sharing your day with other golfers creating beautiful new memories for them and their family along with the precious feeling for the individual of personal worth, self-esteem and achievement.

The combination of social interaction with like-minded people, sharing stories, along with the stimulus created through memory cards combined with a healthy portion of physical activity is the recipe we use to achieve the positive outcomes we have had the pleasure over the years to witness.

Whilst what we do in our group is not a 'cure', the positive and visible impact of making the time to find the right key to unlock an individual's memories is priceless and so extremely rewarding for all.

One day a daughter described to me how she brought a 'gentleman' to the group. The 'gent' was uncommunicative and at times agitated but following the group she took her 'dad' back home. She went on to describe how he was very chatty on the way home; his mood was significantly lifted, and they could once again enjoy a 'father and daughter' relationship. For us, the one tell-tale sign as to his love for golf was that he always wore his golf gloves. That was enough to give us the beginning of a pathway into his memories which clearly showed that for him the physical activity of holding a club and hitting balls was vitally important.

Thanks to everyone for all their golf memories.

Lorraine Young
Chair, Carnoustie Golf Memories

'Why can't I?' – Ian Foggie in his wheelchair

'YES I CAN!' – Ian Foggie on Buddon Links

Preface

BILLY DETTLAFF

It was a typical July Saturday morning. What made it different was televised golf was coming on early, live from Carnoustie, Scotland. It was the third day of play in the 2018 Open Championship. I settled into my burgundy leather recliner ready to watch hours of the action.

Memories of past Open Championships flowed through my mind. I recalled that 56 years earlier, in 1962, ABC transmitted the first live Open telecast to America, using the recently launched Telstar satellite. As a 12-year-old golfer, I cheered on my favourite player, Arnold Palmer, as he captured his second Open title playing over Royal Troon on Scotland's West Coast.

Now, years later, I anticipated seeing great play over the always tough Carnoustie layout. One thing that made watching especially enjoyable was I had played the course in the early 1980s with a group of other golf professionals on a trip to Scotland. I anticipated viewing the event would bring back some great memories.

An hour or two into the coverage, a break in play featured a three-minute segment on the Carnoustie Golf Memories Project. I had no idea the impact the next three minutes would have on me. I learnt that Scotland was the world leader in sports reminiscence therapy and that Carnoustie was the leader in golf programming. *But what did this all mean?*

After taking early retirement in 2009, after 22 years with the PGA Tour's TPC Network, I turned my interests to researching, writing and speaking on the history of the golf profession.

Welcome to

The Pete Dye Chapter
American Golf Memories Project
Presented at TPC Sawgrass
- A Sister Program to the Carnoustie Golf Memories Project Scotland -

In 2016, I self-published *Doctors of the Game*, a 696-page tome on the golf profession. The year before, I was honoured to be

chosen to author the PGA of America's Centennial book. With tears in my eyes after viewing the NBC Golf Memories vignette, I began an online search for the people who appeared in the video. Eventually, I was put in touch with Lorraine Young in Carnoustie, who also made contact for me with Dr Michael Ego of the University of Connecticut. The goal was to learn as much as possible about their programming to see if I could start a programme here in the United States. It seemed a natural extension of my interest in golf history.

Within days I was corresponding with both Lorraine and Michael. I had already planned a speaking tour to Scotland in October, so visiting Carnoustie Golf Memories was a natural extension of that trip. My Scottish host for the visit was Brian Matheson, a fellow golf historian who coincidentally grew up in Carnoustie playing their golf courses. I was pleased that Lorraine was able to reschedule their October meeting so I could attend and participate. Following the meeting, which was filled with typical Scottish hospitality, I was hooked on their programme and the potential of starting one in Florida.

Months of communication followed. Lorraine supplied me with key materials for the organisation and implementation of a programme. I was honoured when Lorraine proposed that we become 'a sister programme' to Carnoustie Golf Memories. Multiple calls with Dr Ego confirmed his passion for these programmes. He had been working with baseball programmes for several years and dearly wanted to see these programmes expanded to golf. His assistance was invaluable.

In December, following a bout with a lung issue that prevented him from flying, Dr Ego and his wife got in their family car and drove to Florida from Connecticut to support me in meetings with two large retirement centres. The idea was to recruit the first members to our Golf Memories club for our inaugural meeting set for the end of January at TPC Sawgrass.

It was surprisingly difficult to recruit individuals to participate. I made two presentations on golf history at retirement centres with a closing pitch for participation in our new American Golf Memories group. There seemed to be a hesitancy from the retirement communities to promote participation, or recognise the value of our program, even after an expert presentation from Dr Ego. Undaunted, we pressed on with our January target. Dr Ego pledged to return to assist in our first meeting.

The staff at TPC Sawgrass, including the general manager, Derek Sprague, the director of golf, Matt Borocz, and the head professional, Brian Riddle, could not have been more supportive of our efforts. They agreed to host our group monthly in one of their golf-themed meeting rooms. I had recently learnt that TPC Sawgrass's course architect, Pete Dye, was in the late stages of Alzheimer's disease. I reached out to his wife, Alice, an equally talented golf course architect, seeking permission to name our programme 'The Pete Dye Chapter' of the American Golf Memories Project. In typical Alice fashion, I received a quick, yet short reply: 'It would be an honour for Pete – Alice Dye'.

On Monday, 28 January 2019, I had only one confirmed participant, Betty Fairchild, a lifelong golfer along with her late husband. At the age of 96, Betty, accompanied by her daughter, Barbara Levine, spoke to me about golf for about an hour. I learnt that she and her husband had travelled the world when he was in the US Air Force. They had even played the Stadium Course at TPC Sawgrass with Barbara and her husband. The three of us had great golf conversations; Betty sharing that her favourite club was a 7-iron. Why? 'It was a versatile club', she said.

Following the meeting, I sent a detailed email to both Lorraine and Michael with a summary of learnt progress. I received a near immediate response congratulating us on the success of our first meeting. Lorraine also supplied a bit of encouragement about the turnout:

> The stigma and fear that is all too often present with regard to dementia is one of the biggest hurdles to overcome. I believe that is the problem for you right now. Once you get even one or two along to the program and word begins to spread about the improvement in their quality of life and general health and wellbeing your membership will grow. The fun, laughter and friendly banter is infectious in the nicest possible way.

A day later, we learnt that our friend and supporter, Dr Ego, had unexpectedly passed away on Sunday, the day prior to the first meeting. Hopefully, he celebrated in knowing his work and dedication brought the first Golf Memories programme to the US.

Over the next couple of months, our group slowly grew in participation. I visited a third retirement and memory care facility where I met Mary Lee Lewis, its programme director. Mary Lee was just the spark we needed for growth. Over the following months, the Pete Dye Chapter grew to 8-10 participants at each meeting. My wife, Geraldine, was called into action to assist with the two-hour sessions.

One of our star participants with a wealth of stories was Billy Maxwell. In 1951, Billy won the US Amateur Championship at Saucon Valley Country Club, Pennsylvania. He went on to win seven titles on the PGA Tour in the 1950s and 1960s. Billy loved our group and sharing his experiences. We were honoured when his daughter, Melanie, chose our September group meeting to host his 90th birthday party. Nearly 100 family members and friends joined the group to celebrate.

One of my favourite meeting memories is the time Billy told the group about when George Zahiris called him to see if he wanted to play a round of golf the next day with himself and his wife, Babe Didrikson Zahiris. Billy made it sound like it was just another day on the course, but this time it was with one of the greatest, longest driving women professionals in history. Unfortunately, we lost Billy on 20 September 2021.

When Covid hit in 2020, we had to postpone further meetings. After a successful twelve-month run, we have been in a two-year hold due to the age and susceptibility of our members. We hope approval to begin our sessions will come soon from retirement facilities. The remarkable camaraderie and storytelling have been missed on all sides.

The relationship between the Carnoustie Golf Memories Project and the American Golf Memories Project – Pete Dye Chapter – continues to fortify. Our shared experiences and learning continue. Here in the US, I stand positioned to share my experiences and materials with anyone interested in creating their own local programme, just as Lorraine and the Carnoustie programme did with me.

The publication of this book serves as an excellent example of our continued support for each other's programmes with a view on future expansion to improve the lives of all golfers challenged with dementia and Alzheimer's disease.

Mind the Links

MICHAEL WELLS

This year (2022) will see the 150th playing of The Open Championship at St Andrews, and what better way to celebrate than recalling memories that the game of golf has provided. Our personal recollections may remind us of some of the great moments that golf's original major, The Open, has given us or we better remember our own clubhouse stories and interactions with Scotland's ancient game, as most golfers enjoy a good yarn.

Michael Wells. CE of Carnoustie Golf Links

Golf must be one of the most sociable sports in the world and is a game that can be enjoyed no matter what your age or ability. Our caddies are custodians of the game and hold archives of stories and advice. I remember asking a caddie if I could get to the green with the 4-iron I was holding, to be told, 'eventually'. Of course, they also have first-hand experience of the Scottish obsession with playing the game quickly and I have heard our starter here at Carnoustie telling players who have jokingly asked what the course record was, to be told deadpan it was 1 hour 56 minutes!

The Open is held on the great Championship Links golf courses of Great Britain and Ireland and was first played for a Moroccan red leather challenge belt, retired after 13 years to be replaced with what is now golf's most coveted and prestigious prize, The Claret Jug. The trophy for golf's original Major has passed through the hands of the greatest to have played the game. From origin championship golfers such as Tom Morris Senior and Junior through the decades and greats such as Arnold Palmer, Ben Hogan and Jack Nicklaus.

I worked for The R&A as part of The Open team for nearly 20 years (my first Open Championship being at Carnoustie in 1999 aged 19), and remember the playoff between Jean van de Velde, Justin Leonard and Paul Lawrie, and the local crowd going wild when Paul hit a glorious shot onto the 18th green to complete the biggest final round comeback in Major championship history.

Carnoustie has a habit of producing drama and rarely lets us down. Back then, The Open seemed huge to me and it was. However, over the next decade it took on a whole new level with enormous change in a brief time. From the explosion in television coverage and commerciality, the rise of the digital age, the modernisation of staging and marketing creating a world-leading sporting event. I can only wonder what those early pioneers would make of the Championship as it is today and the global success it has become since the first ball was struck at Prestwick in 1860.

Tom Watson's 1977 'Duel in the Sun' victory is considered by many to be the finest golf tournament played in the latter half of the twentieth century and over 30 years later he had a global television audience at the edge of their seats as he looked to re-create his emphatic win at Turnberry in 2009, eventually finishing as runner-up to Stewart Cink after a gruelling play off. For me, the emotion in the air that day in 2009 captured the spirit of the game in its purest form, witnessing first-hand one of greats of the game challenging once again for the most sought after of prizes in the same arena but in a different age. You could feel it, the atmosphere was electric. Players, fans, commentators, press and officials all recollecting their own memories of playing golf, watching, and reading about their idols and here was one doing it all again right in front of their eyes. It was a moment for the ages.

At Carnoustie Golf Links we are proud to be a charitable organisation with roots to our local community. We have supported Carnoustie Golf Memories group as they have grown and developed as a leader in supporting those living with dementia and Alzheimer's disease. The collective narratives, poems and recollections in this book bring together a community united by a common good and I am extremely proud to know the pioneers involved with Carnoustie Golf Memories who volunteer their time to support our community and inspire others to do the same.

All the staff at Carnoustie love hosting the group around Links House and consider Lorraine Young and her fantastic Carnoustie Golf Memories team and participants as part of the Carnoustie Golf Links family.

TOTA
STANDARD TEES, 6,701 YARD

16　　MIND THE LINKS – GOLF MEMORIES

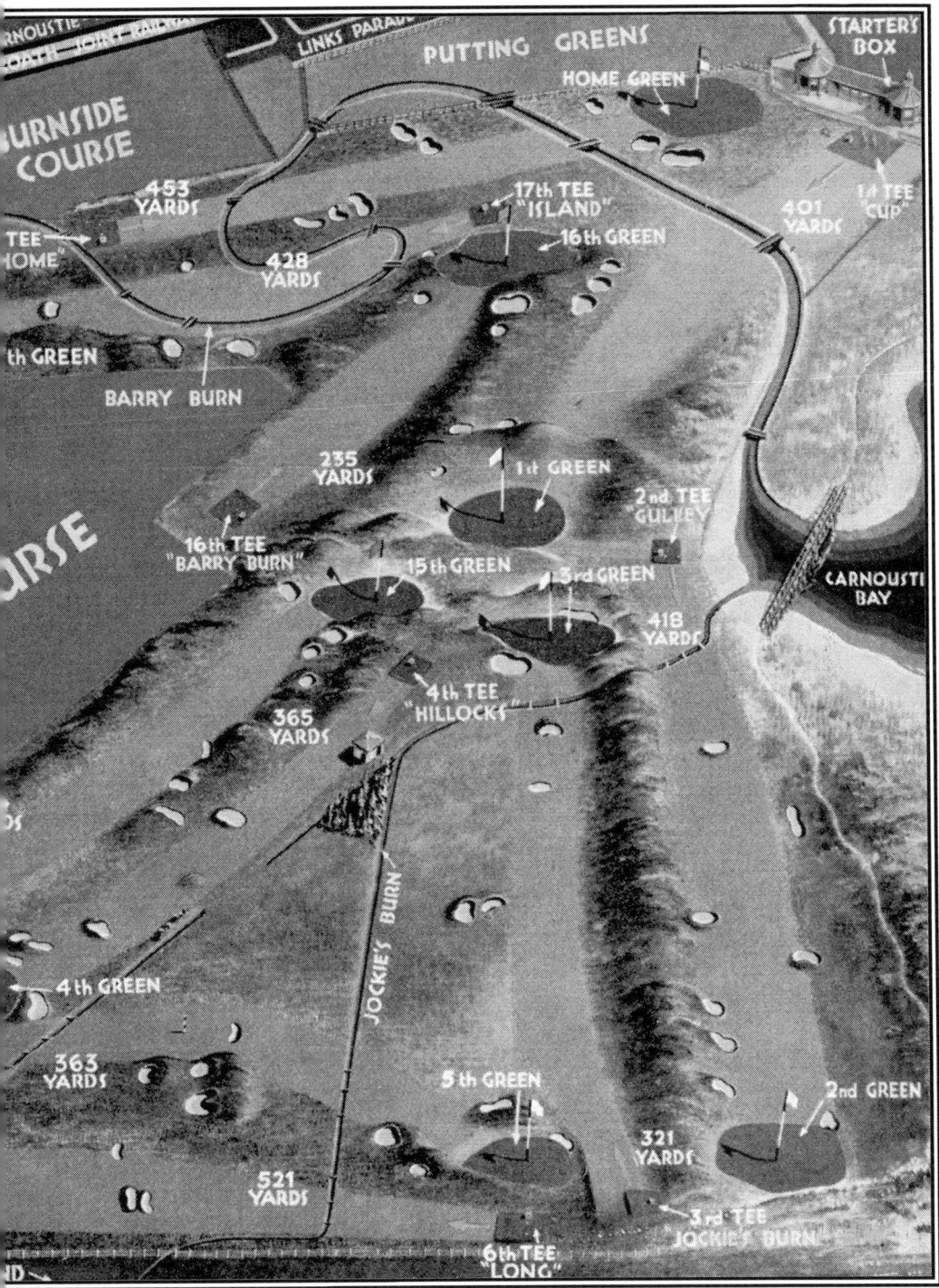

DISTANCE
IGER TEES, 7,200 YARDS

Words of an Open Champion

PAUL LAWRIE

I was born on 1 January 1969 in Aberdeen.

It was brilliant being young. My brother and I both played a lot of football and golf and enjoyed school, but I wasn't very clever so left with no qualifications. I wanted to be a footballer but didn't really have the heart for it and I didn't like tackling, so golf it was!

When Sandy Lyall won at St Georges in 1985, I thought I'm going to be a golfer. My idea was to be a club pro and work in the shop or teach and I would have been perfectly happy doing that. It would be a pretty big dream to think you could go on and make a living or win The Open, but the reality was that I would have been perfectly happy serving the members in the shop or teaching the game. I remember the first day I went into the shop to start work and the pro, Doug Smart, went into the back of the shop and came out with a hoover and a duster and said meet your best friends for the next three years. I'm pretty good at hoovering with all the practice I got when I was young!

I practised almost every single day.

...

The Open in 1999 was at Carnoustie so it was a course that I knew reasonably well. I hadn't organised accommodation for the week of The Open as I didn't know I was playing. I had to qualify to get in and I think I came through with a couple of shots to spare, so I tried to fix up some accommodation after qualifying and there was nothing really close by, but I only lived an hour away, so I thought I'll just stay at home.

Paul Lawrie

Carnoustie's magnificent...That week at The Open in 1999 the rough was very thick and the fairways very narrow, and you could not make a mistake. It was the same for every competitor in the field. As a player it's our job just to get on with it and tackle whatever is put in front of you. Someone's going to win and it's going to be the guy that accepts that's what the challenge is. The best score in round one was level par. I think the cut was 12-over par for the top 65 players, so that shows you how hard the course was playing, when you have the world's best and 12-over par is still there. It was severe, it was tough, but I quite like it that way.

Jean van de Velde was the guy playing the best golf. He was level par for three rounds which, believe me, was incredible golf. He was in pole position, leading The Open by five shots.

The 18th of July 1999 is a day that changed my life and my family's lives forever. I was lying in 13th position, ten shots behind. Colin Montgomerie was ahead of me, Greg Norman, Tiger Woods, Angel Cabrera, Craig Parry and Justin Leonard who had won in 1997. There were a lot of good, seasoned campaigners trying to chase down Mr van de Velde. I got off to a nice start. I was certainly under par early on. You can always tell in a tournament when the crowd starts to swell and the cameras start to appear. I hit a lovely 2nd shot at 12 and I was aware when I was walking down that fairway that there were a lot more people about. At no time was I thinking of winning The Open. I was delighted to be there and delighted to be playing but obviously your name is on the board and the cameras are appearing and you think I'm in this now. You've got an outside chance.

After my round was finished, I'd gone back to the range with my coach, Adam Hunter. From a nearby television, we were witnessing Jean's incredible demise and then he made a brilliant up-and-down just to make it into the play-off with myself and Justin Leonard. On the way to the 15th tee to begin the play-off, Adam told me to look straight into the face of the other two players. He obviously worked out quickly that I was nervous but also knew that they would be too. A complete calmness came over me and my mind was clear. I wasn't thinking about what an opportunity I had, I kind of almost knew I was going to win The Open. I just felt as though I'm going to be The Open Champion right there and then.

Sometimes you've just got to stand up there and hit a good shot and that's what happened. One shot ahead going down the iconic 18th hole, I'd hit a nice tee shot down the fairway and had around 220 yards to the flag. Surrounded by home fans, I selected my 4-iron, got over the ball and straight away a calmness came over me. I wasn't thinking about what it would mean to win the biggest event in the world, I was unbelievably focussed on what I was doing. It came off, a beautiful pure shot. The place went ballistic – it doesn't get any better. My hands were shaking a bit over the putt, but I hit a nice stroke and it went in.

The first time I ever met Jack Nicklaus was in America and he stopped and said, 'Congratulations on winning The Open' and added, 'one of the best shots I've ever seen under pressure'. He patted me on the back and off he went. To take the time to stop and say that. I got a huge lift from that and for him to do that for me, doesn't get any better.

I've never felt anything else but proud of what I've achieved.

The Barry

JIM MACKINTOSH

It was doing what it was supposed to do
weave down through old Carnoustie
mostly unnoticed except for its
solid walled defence
short of the 18th, where that day
he sat down
on the edge of the Barry
on the edge of destiny
first shoes then socks

oh Jean, Jean, Jean
somebody have a word
give him a large brandy
pop him down

into the still of water
knee deep in history, where
in the still of solitude
on the calm side of chaos
just around the hotel corner
Paul Lawrie hunkered over putts
in metro gnomic focus
masking thoughts of what-ifs
what was to become of his destiny
practising what he was supposed to do

Note: *the words in italics were part of Peter Alliss's commentary on the BBC.*

Carnoustie Golf Links, 15 November, 1966

Scottish Golf

GRAHAM BARR

For golfers across Scotland, Gleneagles hosting the 2019 Solheim Cup was a fantastic opportunity to witness some of the best female golfers on the planet going head-to-head in a battle between Europe and the US.

Adding to the occasion was the fact that the European team were captained by Scotland's very own golfing legend, Catriona Matthew.

During her 30-year career, Matthew represented Europe as a player on nine separate occasions, first in 1998 and then for a final time in 2017, missing only one Solheim Cup during that period.

Throughout her nine Solheim Cup playing appearances, Matthew picked up a total of 22 points, making her the third highest points scorer in Solheim Cup history, only behind European legends Laura Davies and Annika Sorenstam. In her final playing appearance in 2017, Matthew picked up an impressive three points, including a 1-up singles victory over Stacy Lewis.

Matthew was also the first Scottish winner of the AIG Women's British Open, claiming the title at Royal Lytham & St Annes in 2009.

With such a distinguished career, she was the ideal candidate to lead Team Europe in the Solheim Cup in her home country at Gleneagles. However, the task was far from an easy one with the US having won the previous two Solheim Cups in 2015 and 2017.

Catriona Matthew. European Solheim Cup win at Gleneagles in 2019

In what was a wonderful week of golf, Europe edged out the US in dramatic fashion by a score of 14.5-13.5.

After three days of fantastic golf, it all came down to the final match, where captain's pick, Suzanne Pettersen, holed a nerve-wracking eight-foot putt to claim victory in her match, and victory overall for the Europeans led by Matthew.

More than 90,000 people attended the event at Gleneagles and for everyone who attended, it was an experience that will live long in the memory, whether that be the amphitheatre that was the first tee, or the celebrations that followed with Matthew and her victorious squad when the winning putt was holed on the 18th green.

Following her successful captaincy in 2019, Matthew once again led the Europeans, this time in Ohio, at the appropriately-named Inverness Club. For only the second time ever, the Europeans were victorious on US soil, giving Matthew her second successive victory as European captain.

In recognition of her services to golf, Catriona Matthew was awarded an MBE in 2010 and then an OBE in 2020.

Michael Ego's Golf and Sports Remembrances

KIMI EGO

My first recollection of my brother and the game of golf was when he was hitting balls with his high school friends at Alondra Golf Course in Gardena, California, in 1966. Who would have thought this day would change his life forever? His love for golf became one of his biggest hobbies. During the next three years, he spent more time at the golf course perfecting his golf swing and watched golf tournaments with Arnold Palmer and Jack Nicklaus rather than hitting tennis balls, his second hobby.

In 1968, he enrolled at California State University, Dominguez Hills in Carson, California. A year later, Michael met Dr John Johnson, the Toros men's head golf coach recruiting students for the university's first collegiate golf team. My brother was ecstatic when he learned he had made the team. The 1969 golf team was the university's first team to compete in intercollegiate athletics, and Dr Johnson left an indelible impression on his life. As a coach and teacher, he encouraged his students 'to also live the life of dreams and that everything was possible if you just believed and did it'.

In 1971, after heeding Dr Johnson's words, my brother became head tennis coach at Dominguez Hills. During his first year, he had a challenging time recruiting tennis players. Most of the students were young, but there was a 60-year-old student who displayed such stamina and athleticism, unlike his younger peers. The curiosity of an older student making the team piqued my brother's interest in pursuing graduate studies in 'Leisure Studies and Recreation' at the University of Oregon, where he took courses on the physical and mental challenges of the ageing population, including studies in dementia and Alzheimer's disease research. After graduating with a PhD in 1980, he continued his research in dementia and Alzheimer's and accepted a position at the American Association of Retired Persons. From 1987 to 1999, he taught classes at California State University in Northridge, California State University in San José and the University of Hawaii in Hilo. In 2005, he accepted an administrative position at the University of Connecticut, Stamford, and later taught classes in the physiological, social, cultural and other aspects of ageing, until 2019.

Since my brother was so impressed with Scotland's successful sports reminiscence programmes, he travelled to Scotland to see first-hand their programmes. In 2017, he befriended Michael White, who graciously took him to see Scotland's sports

Michael Ego (second on the right)

programmes in soccer, golf and shinty, focusing on reminiscence programmes with individuals diagnosed with memory loss and dementia. His visit to Scotland left an indelible impression to implement sports reminiscence programmes in the US.

In 2017, he formed a baseball reminiscence programme at River House Adult Day Center in Cos Cob, Connecticut. River House's clients still attend the Michael Ego Baseball Reminiscence Program, a bi-weekly in-person programme.

In 2018, he met Billy Dettlaff, American Golf Memories Project, Pete Dye Chapter at TPC Sawgrass, and Lorraine Young, Carnoustie Golf Memories Project. The Pete Dye Chapter held its inaugural meeting on 28 January 2019, one day after my brother's passing. Fifty years earlier, in 1969, he played golf with Dr Johnson, his mentor and coach. Who could have imagined these two circumstances would have a monumental impact on my brother's life and career?

My family is profoundly grateful to Billy Dettlaff, Lorraine Young, and Michael White, the creator of Scotland's sports reminiscence programmes and to other individuals who encouraged my brother to implement sports reminiscence programmes in the United States. Today, the programmes are thriving in Connecticut, New York, Texas and California, and plans are to implement more programmes at memory care centres. I continue my brother's baseball reminiscence therapy and volunteer with the Los Angeles Baseball Memories Program and the Baseball Memories Chartered Community Program. In addition, I am virtually attending Michael White's Scotland-based Jukebox Days and Screen Memories Zoom meetings.

(Thank you very much for supporting my brother's sports reminiscence programmes, helping him fulfil his dream, and encouraging him to get involved with programmes focusing on dementia and Alzheimer's.)

Captain of The Royal & Ancient Golf Club of St Andrews

GEORGE McGREGOR

To most people who follow golf closely in both a playing and administration sense the role of the Royal and Ancient (R&A) Golf Club Captain is very much a mystery, that is until, like me, you are fortunate to find yourself part of the process.

Despite having been a member of the club for over 20 years and having played with and been friends of various Captains and past Captains, the selection and process remained very much a mystery to me, in fact a subject which was very rarely discussed.

Over the club's lifetime, which stretches back more than 260 years, there have been various methods used to choose the Captain. In the beginning, the winner of the gold medal automatically became Captain. Being Captain had its downsides: if a member dominated the playing side of the club you were stuck with him and you had to hope that he was acceptable to the club membership!

In recent times, a more businesslike and equitable approach has been adopted whereby past Captains meet in London in early December of the preceding year when their choice is made. In my own case, I was informed by letter the week before Christmas advising of the past Captains' choice. The nomination is kept secret until your name is announced during the business meeting of the spring meeting in May. Your succession begins on the last day of the autumn meeting in September when on the Friday morning the outgoing Captain escorts you down the steps in front of the iconic clubhouse to the first tee for the ritual of driving into office. This dates back well into the nineteenth century.

The experience is made no easier by the fact that you have had four months to think about this event and regardless of your ability there is always the fear that you make a poor stroke. There is only one chance, and you know you are going to be watched by several hundred spectators and supporters, so a well struck drive is required.

Shortly before 8am, the Honorary Professional to the club tees up your ball to the requested height. After a couple of practice swings, you step up to the ball as the clubhouse clock reaches 8am. Hopefully with a solid strike the cannon fires and the caddies, maybe 20 in number, scramble for the ball, the lucky one receiving a gold sovereign as a token from the Captain buying back his ball. During his term in office a silver replica is made of the ball which is then hung on the Silver Club as a record of all the Captains going back to 1754.

Almost as nerve-racking as the drive in is the annual club dinner the same evening which over the last few years has been held in the Fairmont Hotel. There are normally around 500 members present and 20 past Captains. At the dinner, the outgoing Captain presents to the new Captain the Queen Adelaide medal, which was presented to the club by the widow of King William IV, to be worn on all public occasions. Today, a miniature is worn by all past Captains whenever they wear their red coat.

The annual dinner includes speeches by the outgoing Captain and the new Captain, as well as toasts to the new members and a suitable reply. The evening concludes with the annual presentation of trophies, which is a grand occasion.

After the evening was complete and I looked back on a long and very tiring but humble day, the hard work was only beginning for my wife and myself.

Although various past Captains had given us an idea what the year would entail, it was only after meeting with the Captain's Secretary, Karen, that it really came home to us how intense a year this would be. Without Karen's organisational skills, it would have been almost impossible to conduct all the visits and travel that the year entailed.

There is no doubt that over the last few years the R & A along with The Masters Tournament and the United States Golf Association (USGA) have put greater emphasis on the promotion of golf worldwide by taking the game into areas and levels of competition not previously recognised. To enable these initiatives to achieve the desired effect means greater exposure and all this adds to golf's already busy and full calendar.

The Captain's function is very much an ambassadorial role, both at home and overseas as well as being captain of a golf club, which like any other golf club has members who expect their captain to take an active part in the club activities. The R&A has a membership of over 2,000 from all corners of the globe. Many of the overseas members visit during the spring and autumn meetings and are a particularly important asset to the club. During our term, Chrissie and I took part in as many activities within the club as was possible. We got to know the members and enjoyed great support.

If we had been given the choice what year to pick to be Captain, it would have been difficult to improve on our year of 2015 which had so many 'highs'.

To go into the detail of all the events we attended or took part in would take too long. To keep things interesting, I will centre on what we saw as the highlights. This is not to say that every event, whether they be at regional or national level, is not important in its own right; and it is true to say that some of our happiest times where friendships were made took place at lesser-known venues.

To start our year, we had the pleasure of being guests at the Ryder Cup at Gleneagles with a week's stay in the hotel and a grandstand view of all the action. We saw a great win for the European Team over a strong American team. Interestingly, the European Team was captained by Paul McGinley who I had captained in 1991 when he was a member of the Great Britain and Ireland team – how things change!

The following week was the Alfred Dunhill Cup, which is played over three courses: St Andrews – Old Course, Carnoustie and Kingsbarns. It is a 72-hole stroke play tournament to which the R & A Captain gets an invitation to play. I was fortunate to play with Richie Ramsay who finished a very creditable second.

In the coming months, visits were made to Australia, where at Royal Melbourne the Asia Pacific Amateur Championship was played, and a few weeks later, to Buenos Aires for the Inaugural Latin American Amateur Championship, both events supported by the R & A and The Masters Tournament.

For any keen golfer or golf watcher, a trip to The Masters at Augusta must be on their bucket list! We were fortunate to spend the full week there in April with an opportunity to play before the tournament started – a wonderful week. In real life, it is as good, if not better, than it looks on the television.

Another two trips were made to the US. The first was to Sawgrass for the Players Championship, which is known by the players as the fifth Major, and later in the year to Whistling Straits for the PGA Championship – the course was the venue last year for the

Ryder Cup where America overwhelmed Europe. On leaving Whistling Straits, we flew to Winnipeg to attend the Manitoba Golf Association Centenary to fulfil a long-standing promise.

In between these visits to the US, we attended members' gatherings in South Africa and Hong Kong, two quite different countries but with highly active members. In Hong Kong, we attended a major Asian ladies' team tournament which had a long tradition and was very keenly fought!

Through all this travelling, home and amateur golf was not forgotten with visits to various championships and golf clubs. A

George McGregor with 2015 Open Champion Zach Johnson

visit to Stromness in Orkney was one of the most unusual but pleasurable visits. The highlight in team events, however, was at Halmstad in Sweden where Scotland won the men's European Team Championship – all the more pleasing because I was in a winning Scotland team at the same venue exactly 30 years earlier.

As mentioned earlier, to have been chosen to be Captain of the R & A is the greatest honour an amateur golfer can be given. To be fortunate to be Captain in a year when the Open is played at the home of golf – St Andrews – is the icing on the cake.

As well as the playing of the oldest Major in the world, the week is a celebration of golf with visitors from all over the world visiting St Andrews and the Captain participates in many of these activities.

There are two occasions which gave special memories. The first was on the Tuesday evening when a past champions' dinner is hosted in the R & A clubhouse. In 2015, 28 past champions attended and as Captain I hosted and chaired the evening. Attendees included Arnold Palmer and Peter Thomson both now sadly no longer with us. Most other surviving champions attended, and it was an evening that will live with me for ever.

The other occasion was when as Captain I presented the Claret Jug to the winner, Zach Johnston. There are only two Open courses where the R & A Captain presents the trophy, that is Carnoustie and St Andrews where the golf courses are run by a Links trust – at all other venues, the host Club Captain presents the Claret Jug to the winner.

Over the year, there were many happy memories. We travelled extensively and met many wonderful people. One abiding memory is that golf is one big family worldwide and we are so fortunate to be part of it.

The Swilcan

WILLIAM CAINE
First published in *College Echoes*, XVIII, 17 March 1892

Thrice cursed burn, that holdest on thy way
Across the Links with many a twist and turn,
For countless balls, lost in the depths, I pay
      Thrice cursed burn !

Thy gloomy banks, precipitous and stern,
Fill me with quite unutterable dismay:
And when they sluggish waters I discern,

For just one good approach shot I will pray;
And trust that in the future I may learn
To pass thee safely, after years of play,
      Thrice cursed burn!

Jack Niklaus waving from the Swilcan Bridge

On the Road

PAUL FORSYTH

On paper, the nuts and bolts of the Road Hole at St Andrews would not be out of place among the windmills and shipwrecks of Paradise Island. Blind tee shot, left-to-right around a five-star hotel. The Sands of Nakajima protecting a sliver of green that is almost impossible to catch. And the eponymous road behind, where punters gather to peer over the wall at an unfolding circus.

The St Andrews Old Course road hole during the Walker Cup

Crazy golf? You bet it is, but the 17th at the Old Course didn't become the toughest par 4 in the world, the most iconic, most historic challenge in golf, without also being one for the purists. Strip back the 495-yard challenge to its bare essentials and you have a stretch of land like no other in the game, one that will attract scrutiny, head-scratching and its usual share of admiration at this summer's 150th Open Championship.

Just ask Stephen Gallacher, the Scottish professional, who won the 2004 Alfred Dunhill Links Championship at the Old Course and has played it more than most. When he arrives on the tee, with the sea to his left, the Royal & Ancient Clubhouse ahead and the town disappearing behind the Old Course hotel, he thinks about the hole's past and the honour of playing there, but he also thinks about how the hell he is going to get a par. 'Yes, it's got a road', he says.

> It's got a bunker. It's got a hotel and a pub…and a shed. That all sounds a bit gimmicky, but it's far from it. It's one of the great golf holes. The crack with the boys is that it's the best par 5 in the world…it's so tough. Since they put the tee back 35 yards, it's been even harder. It's nearly 500 yards: a drive and a 3-iron, maybe a 2-iron. It's a proper hole, up there with some of the most demanding in the world.

As seasoned observers will know, the ideal strategy is to drive over what was once a railway shed – it juts out into the crook of the dogleg – and to do it so bravely that you flirt with the out-of-bounds hotel. That allows an approach to the front right of the putting surface, which is guarded by the dreaded Road bunker. The last place to be is in or short of the sand, where the mind-messing lob to a slender green can all too easily find tarmac through the back.

That, though, is not to take account of the weather, changing pin positions and the whim of the more imaginative golfer. 'The thing I love most about the hole is that there are so many ways to play it', adds Gallacher.

> I've seen guys hit tee shots down the second fairway, I've seen them bumping and running it, leaving it short, and I've seen them hitting on to the side of the first green so that it leaves an easy chip up. It's basically doing anything to avoid that bunker or hitting it long. That's your nemesis.

The history of the Road Hole is humbling. While it has since become a template replicated all over the world, it was not inspired by the work of a genius architect. In fact, it was a product almost entirely of nature, one that was adapted for the game's development. Before the 1870s, golfers plotted their way round clockwise, playing eleven holes out and back. And what is now the 17th was at that time two holes – the third and fourth.

Roger McStravick, the golf historian who specialises in all things St Andrews, says the hole we know now, like much of the Old Course, needed little or no intervention by man. 'The whole back nine was almost created by God', he says.

> Golf has been played there since the 1400s. It was just natural. The bunkers were natural. That's where the cows bunked, where they slept. So that's where the phrase comes from.

At one stage, there was a plan for the current first green to be that of the 17th, which would have given the course's penultimate challenge a direct path across the links. Thank goodness it never happened. The hole in its current form has been notorious since the day in 1885, when a chap named David Ayton, five shots clear in The Open, reached the edge of the green in two. He pitched on to the road, back into the bunker, needed five to escape and two-putted for an eleven. He missed a playoff by two strokes.

Not much in the folklore of golf has attracted more attention than the Road bunker, a devilish pot that seemed to grow deeper over the years, hollowed out by hapless players digging deep, and tourists posing for a holiday snap. Some of its height was taken away in 2002, but if the ball is close to the face and the sand is raked flat, a shot to the green feels all but impossible. The list of victims is long and legendary, from David Duval and Constantino Rocca to Ernie Els and the fictional character buried there in Angus MacVicar's *Murder at The Open*.

But the player whose name has become synonymous with it is Tommy Nakajima. He was tied for the lead in the third round of the 1978 Open when his putt across the treacherous green caught the wrong slope and trickled into the sand. He needed four shots to escape, signed for a nine and was asked later if he had lost his concentration. 'No', he replied. 'I lose count'.

Then there is the road and, more specifically, the wall that runs alongside it, an 'immovable obstruction' from which there is no relief. When Tom Watson pushed his approach so close to it that he could only jab his ball onto the green and make bogey, it cost him a playoff in the 1984 Open. Others have opted to punch it against the dyke and hope upon hope that they land on the putting surface, as Miguel Angel Jimenez did in 2010.

The green itself is a hair-raiser. There were shades of Nakajima about Rory McIlroy in the 2014 Alfred Dunhill Links Championship. He was tied for the lead when his putt over the back of the bunker slowed up too quickly and dropped into the sand. The Northern Irishman got up and down in two, but the bogey meant that he finished a stroke behind Oliver Wilson.

Nowhere in the world does a hole have so many famous features. The hotel, which needs reinforced windows and rubber roof tiles to deal with errant shots, is where a railway station used to stand. The *Jigger Inn,* to which players retire for a pint or three, was the stationmaster's house. The shed that blocks out half the view from the tee is where they used to store golf-club hickory, delivered by passing trains. 'There's a book to be written on that alone', says McStravick.

> It's where they dried the hickory wood. At one stage, they took the shed down, but there was an outcry so they put up a replica. With the shed there, you are not sure if you are in or out of bounds. And that's the joy of it.

For the drive, players identify one of the town's steeples as their line. Before the tee was relocated in a nearby practice area, they picked out the words, or even letters, on the side of the shed. Which 'o' they chose in 'Old Course Hotel' was a measure of their courage. 'The writings on the wall', said Nick Faldo, the former Open champion, who might as well have been referring to the sense of doom with which players address the task.

It is a potential card-wrecker that preys on the minds long before it hoves into view. No matter how few strokes it has taken to cover 16 holes, or how much fun has been had in the process, it counts for nothing until the day's biggest hurdle has been overcome. Gallacher has never had a birdie there. In the 2010 Open, he was a cumulative six-over par on the 17th, a total that he reckons cost him a top-ten finish.

It doesn't suit the shape of Gallacher's shot, but he will never allow that to cloud his judgment of the Road Hole. He loves drinking in the *Jigger,* staying in the hotel, drawing back the curtains and stepping onto the balcony for a view that he says is 'like Disneyland for golfers'. But most of all he loves its authenticity, its natural strengths and the effortless way it and the rest of the course have given so much to so innocent a patch of coastline.

It's just that bit of land from the sea that nobody wanted to farm, says Gallacher.

That's what the links were – a link to the mainland. It's a proper experience, the Old Course. If I could only play one course for the rest of my life, it would be that place. Because it changes daily. The 17th changes daily. You could play it 50 different ways if you wanted. And that, I think, is the mark of a great hole.

But the Sea is

LARISSA REID

I fancied my footprints fossilised on this shore;
A youngster clasping tight to seashells,
Filling buckets and bailing sea from makeshift moats,
Tumbling headfirst through white caps,
While the helicopters birled overhead.

A long-distance cloup of golf shots
And the crowd roars like the North Sea waves;
The TV commentators laugh at the daft ones
Swimming in that water.
I smile;
You think you're in charge, I whisper,
But the sea is.

The flags pinioned to the St Andrews' skyline
Flick and twist in a sudden lifting breeze.
The growling haar, rolling like a grey seal onto its back,
Sighs and furls further away out to sea,
Leaving the sun to stretch over green and fairway.

The crowd ripples and lifts and settles,
Like the dunlins on the tide line,
Following the drives and putts,
The bunker shots and rough rescues,
Picking over perfect scores
And fluttering polite congratulations.

The players take their chances with the shifting rainbows;
Hoping the course doesn't slide back into the
   otherworld,
Before the shimmering July light fades.

And the daft one in the water?
Aye.
That was me.

Walking with Sandy, Seve and Dad

PETER ROY

Pick up any golf magazine shortly before The Open and you will read of players past and present excitedly plotting their annual pilgrimage to play links golf. 'Experience' is a much relied upon catchword in these articles together with 'subtlety' and 'nuance'. But I've long held the belief that the players' experience disregards so many of the important intricacies that we, the mere mortals, navigate at this wonderful tournament.

While the players can tell you how to navigate the valley of sin, Hell bunker, and Duncan's Hollow, or how to hold the ball against a tricky right to left wind, they don't know which Open venue's hospitality tent provides the best bacon sandwich (my dad can give a precise and detailed explanation as to why it was Turnberry in 2009). They can't tell you exactly which stand provides the optimum view across multiple holes at an Open venue (the golf viewing aficionados' Shangri-La) or how to navigate the order of play with surgical precision to ensure you time your day to see all of your favourite players.

My introduction to The Open began on a warm practice day at Royal Troon in 1989 (yes, I still have my ticket and programme). For some, it may be a beautiful F1 car, and for others a great song or painting that fires their imagination but for me it was that first day at The Open. Walking through the tented village and over to the practice range with dad, mum, and my sister I was instantly captivated. Watching my soon to be hero, Sandy Lyle, hitting 1-irons, Seve warming up next to him with his wedges, the artistry and skill of both was magical.

So inspired was I with The Open that I begged my dad to take me on two of the competition days later that week, and it delights me to say we have attended almost every Open together since (ill-timed weddings and graduations permitting).

While The Open has given me a never diminished love of our great game, there is another wonderful gift that it has bestowed and that is the fantastic days spent beside my dad at each Open venue, discussing not only bacon sandwiches and great shots but life, the universe, Partick Thistle and everything in between. I'll treasure those moments forever.

This year The Open celebrates 150 years of competition, and with it comes an exciting landmark for me too. I will be there, at St Andrews, with my dad and my mum, my wife and my two sons. It will be a truly special moment and it's my hope that my boys are as inspired as I was on that Wednesday in mid-July 1989.

Est-ce que vous Jouez au Golf?

My Golfing Life

PATRICIA SAWERS

It's in the genes or it's in the blood.

Being brought up in a golfing family and living in Carnoustie, I was introduced to the 'honourable game' at an early age. Playing golf gave me a wonderful grounding for life: it taught me manners, patience, discipline and, most of all, involved making friends which have lasted a lifetime.

Patricia Sawers, Carnoustie Golf Links Management Committee

The Championship course at Carnoustie is recognised globally as iconic within golfing circles, the direction of every hole changing around each point of the compass. It is renowned for hosting many amateur and professional championships; with my first real memory being The Open Championship in 1968 when I was ten. I remember the area around the Links being transformed from an open green space to become a coating of white tents, my first introduction to a tented village.

Watching the 'Black Knight', Gary Player, winning the Championship and lifting the Claret Jug was awe inspiring. In 1975, as a teenager I saw The Open return to the town. Carnoustie was turned into a vibrant eclectic town with its golf clubs, bars and restaurants filled with fun, merriment and tales of wayward drives and missed putts. It saw the first of Tom Watson's five Open Championship wins.

It was after this the Carnoustie courses saw a steady decline in condition and, in 1979, the establishment of the Carnoustie Golf Links Management Committee (CGLMC) with my uncle, Dougal Thomson, appointed as its first chairman. The full committee was made up of two representatives from the six constituent golf clubs within Carnoustie. The aim of the CGLMC was to see the return of the Links to championship condition and secure the return of prestigious championships. In 1983, my father, Ron Bell, joined the committee as greens convenor. Being a farmer, he worked closely with John Philp the Links Superintendent to bring the courses back to their glory with the prospect of Major championships returning. In 1995 and 1996, Carnoustie hosted the Scottish Open and also received the news all had been waiting for: the return of The Open in 1999 after a 25-year gap.

Carnoustie has seen many prestigious winners over the years, but the 1999 Open will long be remembered not for the outstanding play of Scot Paul Lawrie but for the spectacular collapse of Jean Van de Velde who standing on the 18th tee with a three-shot lead was in everyone's mind 'the winner'. His final hole with the image of him taking off his socks and shoes and thinking seriously of stepping into the Barry Burn to play his shot as the water rose around his ankles will be etched in my mind for ever. Standing at the back of the green watching this unfold was indeed history in the making. After this event, Carnoustie gained the unfortunate title of 'Carnasty' due to the long, thick, rough, narrow fairways, and the natural elements of wind and rain. I don't believe it was 'Carnasty' – it was a true test of links golf. Back on The Open Championship rota we made a promise we would never allow Carnoustie to fall back into the wilderness years of 1975-1999.

My journey of playing golf continued but I also wanted to give back to the sport and the town I loved. I became a director of CGLMC in 2010, following in the footsteps of my uncle and father. In 2014, I became Chairman of CGLMC, a year in which I oversaw the organisation become a charitable trust. It was also the year in which The R&A announced the return of The Open in 2018. Sadly, at this time my father was diagnosed with dementia so when Lorraine Young approached me with the idea of setting up a group to support people with memory loss through golf, I was delighted to provide my wholehearted support and Golf Memories Carnoustie was established. Carnoustie Golf Links is still immensely proud to support the work of the group.

As Chairman of CGLMC, it was a huge honour to host the British Amateur Championship in 2015 won by Romain Langasque, the Senior Open in 2016 won by Paul Broadhurst and the 2018 Open won by Francesco Molinari. The silver medal in 2018 was won by Scotland's Sam Locke. Let's hope he goes on to be as successful as Rory McIlroy who won the silver medal at Carnoustie in 2007.

Since becoming a charity in 2014 the Links has given in excess of £250,000 to community groups and charities in the area. It provides free junior golf to local schools and currently has around 300 children in the golf development programme and is also running a very successful programme aimed at introducing women to golf.

I stepped down as Chairman of Carnoustie Golf Links in 2021 but am very proud of what the organisation accomplished during my eight years at the helm – to develop a sustainable organisation, to support and develop the staff and ensure that as a charitable trust we continue to give back to the local community.

I look forward to watching the next chapter of Carnoustie Golf Links.

A young Patricia Sawers playing golf in her garden

The Caddy

JENNIE TURNBULL

I was your caddy, aged three,
too small to carry the bag
more there for company
a tic tac to keep me sweet;
every second tee,
handing you an iron,
putting on the green,
lifting the pin to let the ball drop in.

I was your caddy, a sulky fifteen,
torn between my dad
and the friends I'd rather be;
slowly unbending from green to green,
to talk, or just walk
in quiet company;
learning where to stand,
what to watch for, how to be,
lifting the pin to let the ball run in.

I am no golfer,
nor shall ever be,
but you have been my caddy
from the very first tee;
not choosing my direction,
but advising how to aim,
mostly patiently explaining
and waiting,
again and again.

Lifting my bag when the hole is too long,
the rattle of tic tacs from your pocket when my energy is low,
applauding my success as if it were your own,
a loving arm across my shoulders as we turn for home.

Bob Hope with caddy at Carnoustie, 1952

Some Memories

TREVOR WILLIAMSON

I consider myself to be a lucky person. I have had a life which has been full of coincidences, resulting in many stories to be told!

When I was a wee boy of four or five, my mum and I would come back from Edinburgh to the Simpson family home, *Rockliff*, for a holiday. My dad was from Edinburgh, and we lived in Fairmilehead. A great treat for me was when my Auntie Gertie took me along to the golf shop. I couldn't wait to get through to the back shop where the clubmakers worked. To me as a wee boy, they seemed like giants, not ogres, but strong friendly giants. At that time, there were two, Jock Brown and Willie Smart. The first time I saw them they became my heroes; they'd hoot with laughter when they handed me the heavy wooden mallet. *'Here you hold that young Trevor.'* The weight and size of this tool nearly pulled me through the floor, like a cartoon character! Willie Smart was my main hero, constantly doing remarkable things. On a dark December night just before Christmas, Willie ventured on to the golf course and cut down a tree from the plantation at the 3rd hole. This was not something that would have gained the approval of Carnoustie Links Committee, but when these trees were put up in the parlour at *Rockcliff*, they were the best Christmas trees ever. Willie gave me my first golf lessons, and it was he that took me out in his fishing boat in the dangerous North Sea, my mum watching from the drawing room window. It was a shame: using her binoculars, she thought that the boat had gone down, but it had only vanished behind waves. When I returned, it was made quite clear I would not be allowed out on The German Ocean in the near future. I was not scared at all that day; it is amazing how safe you can feel when you are in the company of friendly giants!

The memories that never left me are the smells of the workshop back then. The sweet smell of spirit varnish, the leather of the golf grips, a smell of its own, not like shoes or anything else. There was also the smell of pitch, and gas from the simmering lead ladle.

Rockcliff

When I was five, mum and dad split, so mum and I came to stay in *Rockcliff.* That was paradise for me – 14 rooms in which to hide and doting aunts and uncles to spoil me, as well as beach, golf and great summers.

...

When the First World War came along, to avoid being called up, many of the clubmakers faked injury by bandaging hands and so on. They were neither conscientious objectors nor cowards, but they loved working for Mr Simpson and being out on the golf course on a summer's night, playing with clubs they no doubt made themselves. As one gets older and gets a bit more cynical, the play back then seems to have been much closer to nature. The golfer, as always, is taking on the elements, wind, rain, hot sun (sometimes) but, moreover, taking on these elements with the wood of the hickory shafts, persimmon heads, lead for weight, leather for grips, natural materials, not a tin can for a head, a plastic shaft and a rubber grip – that's me being cynical!

There is a story about one of these young men and his name was David Fearn. David was learning to be a clubmaker at Simpson's. He stayed outside Arbroath, with his mother and father at a cottage at what was known as the 'Three Mile Wood' about five miles from his work. Bob Simpson would sometimes stand outside with his pocket watch, awaiting Fearn's arrival on his bicycle; he best not be late. David thought it best to sign up and go and fight for his country. My mother, who I think might have had a crush, said he was great at whistling a tune. A lot of men had no notion about the horrors to come. David wrote to my grandmother Janie Simpson from the front in France, he said how wonderful it must be back in Carnoustie now that summer was there, he was missing being on the golf course, he also told how the officers had given them footballs, and they had great fun having a game. He also talked about the 'The Hun had good aim yesterday, hit the Forfarshire up the road' almost a game. A year later, at 19, the bereavement appeared in the local paper. David is buried in the British Indian cemetery in France.

...

The Simpson Brothers, The Links, Carnoustie, 1885

When I was ten, The Open arrived at Carnoustie. This was a time of great excitement: Ben Hogan's first and only Open, and he won it. Stars everywhere, Frank Sinatra. Bing, all the world's best golfers, Roberto Vicenzo and Tony Cerda kept their clubs at *Rockliff*, new heroes! Prompted by my auntie, I sold my first golf ball, my first transaction in golf! I always loved hanging about the golf shop, annoying whoever was working there! Five years later, I left school and started working in the golf shop. My uncle Bob, son of Robert, taught and gave me my first lessons in golf club making. I am so grateful for this. At the time, I would rather have been playing with my chums, but when I made and sold my first set of irons, I thought, 'This is for me'. I have done just about everything in golf. I was a caddy when I was 16; the starter would phone up and ask mum if I was available. In those days, there were few overseas visitors and about six caddies. Now there are thousands of visitors and 200 caddies. One day, I was asked to caddie for a lady who was the Italian Open Champion. At the second hole, she asked me the yardage to the pin. As all of us just played by instinct and feel, I told her I didn't know. This did not go down very well, I know this because at the end of the round, she asked, 'Do you know the name and phone number of any good caddies in Carnoustie?'

I never went to caddie again for about 35 years, too embarrassed. I did go back and enjoyed it very much. To do this job properly, you must be a mother or father figure, firm but sympathetic, very, very understanding.

I have worked on hundreds of golf clubs, and some for Arnold Palmer, Tom Weiskopf, and many others. Golf has taken me to America nearly 30 times, I have met so many great people, and made several films. My greatest honour was to be made 'Ambassador and Keeper of the Carnoustie Way'.

The town of Carnoustie has made the biggest contribution to golf than any other, I am happy if I can let the world know something about that.

...

As the twentieth century approached, things began to change. The ordinary men and women were keen to play, and public golf courses would help to make this happen. In the bygone days of the Feather Golf Ball, 'The Feathery', the cost of a ball was prohibitive, but the coming of the Gutta Percha Ball, changed all that. 'The Gutty' as it was known was cheap and easy to make, and if they broke, could be remoulded. The making of golf clubs was a very skilled profession, the maker had to be a very competent woodworker, but apart from being a thing of beauty, it had to be an asset to the golfer, for just as today, players wanted to hit the ball further and straighter. Early golf clubs are things to wonder at. Club makers like the McEwan family, and the man known as 'The Chippendale' of golf clubmakers, Hugh Philp, were makers of the most elegant golf clubs. So, as golf ball production was keeping up with demand and improvements and ideas to 'help' the golfer's game were coming thick and fast, now the clubs had to catch up. The first stage for making the head for a wooden golf club was hard. It would be freed from a block of beechwood, and later persimmon. This would then be filed and worked on, until all the correct angles and shapes were achieved. A machine that had been used for years to make such things as shuttles for jute mills, tool handles, and other wooden items was brought into the club-making workshop. Known as a copying lathe, the machine would have one or two masters at one side. These would be made of bronze or brass, on the other side would be fitted wooden 'boots' as they were called. Cutters would follow the shape dictated by the masters turning the 'boots' into a roughly shaped head. The lathe could produce hundreds of these in a day. This sped up production, but the skill and artistry had still to be there. So much interest was attached to golf, that when my grandfather, Robert Simpson, bought a second engine to power one of these, the story went into the newspapers! It also gives an idea how many clubs were being produced, that he needed two copying lathes, but the quality was always the best.

...

Great Britain at that time had a strong class society. If a visitor had arrived at Carnoustie Links in let us say 1900, they would see more than a half-dozen golf clubhouses. The main ones were situated on Links Parade, and they are as follows:

The Dalhousie Golf Club (est. 1868) – This was a very impressive building, with towers and an almost castle-like appearance. It was the club of landowners and top businessmen from the nearby city, in other words the upper classes. This was the club that ran the course. In the early days, they had the power to get things done, they were determined that the lands known as the Links would be for all to enjoy for all time.

Travelling from east to west, the next clubhouse would be the **Carnoustie Golf Club (est. 1842)**. This was an artisan/working-class club. The members here would be tradesmen, joiners, plumbers and, yes, golf clubmakers.

A few yards further west is the **Caledonia Golf Club (est. 1886)**. The members of this club were bankers, insurance men, in short, a middle-class membership.

The last club in Links Parade (last but by no means least) is the **Carnoustie Ladies Golf Club (est. 1873)**. This date makes this the oldest ladies golf club in the world. The game of croquet was popular with the gentle ladies back then, playing in their finery on a sunny summers evening. The ladies of Scotland, however, decided that being fit and healthy was becoming desirable. They saw that being out in the bracing sea air, and using hitherto unused muscles, that was not only good for their wellbeing, but they would enjoy the competition. Women have always played a great part in golf here at Carnoustie, and still do.

The other clubs in town are:

The New Taymouth (est. 1906), which was more a social club but with a strong golfing membership.

The Mercantile Golf Club (est. 1896), which was founded by Carnoustie's shopkeepers. In bygone days, shops had what was known as a half-day. In the City of Dundee, it was Wednesday, in Carnoustie, it was Tuesday; so, at midday, shops closed, and off to the course!

The Station Masters Golf Club (est. 2006) is a charitable organisation, and highly active. As was often the way before golf clubs had their own buildings, the members would meet at a local inn. In this tradition, the members of this club conduct their business in the *Station Hotel*. While not all the original clubhouses stand, things have not changed that much. Carnoustie's golf courses are, as they have always been, public golf courses.

Local golfers join the club that suits them best, or that in which their friends are members. Each club conducts its own business, catering, competitions etc. All the golfers pay for what is known locally as a 'Season Ticket', which allows them to play on the wonderful Carnoustie courses – The Championship, The Burnside, The Buddon Links and The Nestie. The Nestie is a 6-hole junior course that is free to members and non-members. Clubs are available at the pro-shop. So, grandad can take the youngsters on and show them how it is done.

The beauty of the system is the locals and the visitors share the courses. It is truly 'Golf for All' at Carnoustie.

In 1842, Alan Robertson of St Andrews laid out a 10-hole course at Carnoustie. It is believed that he created a 7-hole layout before that. Robertson was deemed to be the first golf professional. He was a legendary feather golf ball maker and clubmaker. It was with Robertson that Tom Morris (Old Tom) was to serve his apprenticeship, until they had a big fallout (but that's another tale!).

In 1872, the Dalhousie Golf Club requested Tom Morris to inspect the Carnoustie course to see what improvements he might see as possible. The next year, in May 1873, following Morris's advice, Carnoustie opened its 18-hole golf course.

The next move by the Dalhousie Golf Club, while they could not have predicted it, would change the path of golf forever. In August 1883, Robert Simpson of Earlsferry was given the job as clubmaker at the Dalhousie Golf Club (Carnoustie course). He would be required to teach, repair and make clubs for members (and balls), play in tournaments, be curator of the course and organise the caddies. Robert served his apprenticeship with Robert Forrestor of Elie/Earlsferry, and before Carnoustie, Robert Forgan of St Andrews. One of six golfing brothers, Robert's skill in designing and making golf clubs soon became world renowned. He worked with Tom doing alterations at Carnoustie; he and Morris did the original plans for Carnoustie's second course. In their working life, the Simpson brothers did amazing things: they designed golf courses, Jack Simpson was Open Champion at Prestwick in 1884, Archie Simpson was second the year after – the Simpson name showed more than any other in The Open top places back then.

...

There were several golf club makers in Carnoustie at the turn of the 1900s: Walter Hewitt, Charles Brand and Robert Simpson were the best, but the standard was high with them all. To work with Simpson was the best. There was never a golf professional, nor is there likely to be another, like Robert 'Bob' Simpson. I talked earlier about the class structure, but that didn't apply to

Bob Simpson or his wife Janie. When a young Winston Churchill was campaigning in nearby Dundee, he stayed with Bob at *Rockcliff*. He was also a colleague of Sir Arthur Conan Doyle, of Sherlock Holmes fame. And when the young men who stood at the Simpson club-making benches were called to fight in the Great War, it was Janie Simpson they wrote letters to from the trenches in France. And when Robert died in 1923, it was golf club makers that were the pallbearers.

If a young man showed he was keen and showed promise, then his life might change forever. It is true they would be taught club-making skills to the highest standard, but Bob Simpson also taught them how to get on in life and in business. They saw how Mr Simpson had got on, after all he now had a bigger house than some of the men that originally employed him! Most importantly, however, they might get the chance to work in golf in another land. And so they did, over 300 young lads went all over the world, but the majority went to the USA, taking with them their skills in golf club making, green keeping, course design, teaching, playing in championships and everything else golf-wise.

A famous golf writer once wrote, 'There is not a country in the world that you won't find an "R Simpson Made in Carnoustie" golf club. He could have said, 'There is not a golf course in the USA you won't see a Carnoustie man'. These men were also involved in the formation of the USPGA, the Australian PGA and many others.

Alex Smith was a foreman with Bob Simpson. When he was asked if he would recommend a good man for a position in the USA, Bob Simpson had had no hesitation in putting Smith forward. The 1906 and 1910 US Opens were won by Alex; his brother, Willie, had won the 1899 US Open, and the legend that was Macdonald Smith was already out there. So over 300 men departed and began this new and exciting life in the 'Land of Promise'.

Stewart Maidens, taught by Archie Simpson, was the creator of the 'Carnoustie Swing', which is how all these different skills went around the world. It was the case that you had to have a Carnoustie man at your golf club.

I am proud that Robert Simpson was my grandfather and proud that Jack, Archie, Alex, David and Charles were my great-uncles. When the likes of the Simpsons took on their St Andrews counterparts in the Grand Matches, the Smiths, Maidens etc would get to caddie for their heroes and see close up how it was done – how wonderful that must have been for them.

When I was a wee boy, like Bobby Jones, I followed the likes of Doug Dalziel and Wallace McArthur round the Championship course at Carnoustie. They soon would leave for America, the last of the 'Carnoustie 300'.

A Round on the 'Big' Course & Pic of the Day

DONALD FORD

In the last decade of the twentieth century, I was taking the photographs and writing the editorial for an annual publication covering everything within Scottish golf. I featured one of The Open Championship courses each year, and Carnoustie was my selection for the next golfing handbook.

At that time, Colin Sinclair was the Carnoustie Links professional, so I contacted him to see if I might accompany him on a round of the 'big' course, in the expectation of getting a professional view of how to handle (without doubt) the hardest links in The Open Championship.

So it transpired that, at 6am one spring morning, I found myself on the first tee with Colin, notebook and pen suitably available for all the do's and don'ts which applied if the great course was to be overcome. It would be an understatement to simply say that it all went well. Colin's relentless, superb ball striking was just brilliant, while his hole-by-hole observations were hugely educational for a very average player like myself – and readers, of course.

Fast forward, therefore, to the sixteenth tee, from which even The Open Champion in 1975, Tom Watson, could not collect *one* par from four attempts on this quite extraordinary 'short' hole. As I completed my notes from Colin's comments on the fifteenth green, he struck a tremendously long iron shot, with his ball coming to a halt just a few yards below the flag. My drive was reasonably well struck but found the horrendous bunker to the front right of the green.

So we set off, with Colin yielding more pertinence to the importance of choosing the right club, then striking the ball perfectly to leave par putting a formality. As we walked down the fairway, I noted the approach of someone from the first fairway. It turned out to be Links Superintendent John Philp, whose tireless work since 1985 had brought Carnoustie back to where it certainly belonged – on The Open rota.

John Philp MBE. Links Superintendent at Carnoustie 1985-2012

Picture the scene, as I disappeared into the front bunker with my sand wedge. With a degree of skill which I never believed was in me, my bunker shot cleared the fierce sand cliff above the ball, headed greenwards…and, to my astonishment, was greeted by a sincere 'Brilliant shot, Donald' from Colin. While I raked the sand in the bunker, he casually knocked his twelve-foot putt into the hole. To this day, the apparent simplicity of his birdie remains outstanding.

Donald Ford. Scottish landscape and golf photographer

He had, graciously, rolled my own ball (just a few feet from the hole) back to me as I reached the green after my repairs to the sand. By this time, John had come down to greet us. He congratulated Colin on a great birdie. I too, of course, was more than delighted at securing something that Tom Watson never even sniffed in 1975.

I had a broad smile on my face as John approached me. I was anticipating a message from him on my own success. 'Donald', he said quietly, 'could you please go back and sort that sand in the bunker? You've made a right mess of it'. The perfectionist at his best. What a great memory...to this day!

...

Then, there was a quite astonishing incident on the second green at Royal Dornoch. I had chosen to photograph its magnificent links, given a promise of fine summer weather early in the morning. My four-hour drive of some 200 miles from Carnoustie found me on the course at 6am. The forecast of a fine start to the day was spot-on.

The reason for the visit was to capture a few more photographs of the legendary course, ideally for publication in the following year's golf calendar. Since it had first been distributed at the end of the twentieth century, my customer numbers had increased year on year. In 2010, around 25 customers were from America's western states, two of whom, Bob and Claire Erskine, had been devoted Californian customers from the very first edition.

Those who know this great layout will be aware of the right-angled turn after some seven holes. On the way back, the green on the short tenth offered a brilliant composition in superb early sunshine. Pic of the day? Undoubtedly...so, the long walk back to the clubhouse began.

Two or three additional photographs were captured before I reached the slope up to the rear of the second green. Two golfers were heading my way from the tee. Both balls were well placed on the green. I stopped to allow the couple to putt out... two pars rewarded the pair (one lady, one gentleman) for their excellent tee shots.

I picked up my tripod, backpack and camera bag before restarting the walk back to the clubhouse. The male golfer was passing me on his way to the third tee. He stopped. 'Donald Ford?', he asked with a clear American accent. 'Yes...that's me', I replied. 'Bob and Claire Erskine', he blurted out excitedly! I was thunderstruck, three mouths opened wide in amazement, and hugs and handshakes were vigorously exchanged.

The astonishment and quite nonsensical chance of us meeting up at this moment are just ludicrous. These husband-and-wife golfers were 5,000 miles from home. The photographer had driven 200 miles from Carnoustie over four hours. Had a bookmaker been present, and given the enormity of the circumstances on the possibility of the threesome meeting up, what on earth would his odds have been on the likelihood of a liaison on this far-flung golf links?

Such an astonishing combination of travel, timing and utter coincidence *must* surely be unique?

A shot of the 10th at Royal Dornoch

Carnoustie Links

PATRICK HEALY

When thumbing through the *Concise Collins*
I came across the term 'pilliwinks',
A mediaeval instrument of torture
A reminder of my favourite links.
Yet meet this lady when it's calm
With all her beguiling charms laid bare,
Just tame her on a windless day
You are better than the average player.

Past burn and bunker to the green
The ball is flying straight and far,
You begin to think this course is easy
As you sink your second putt for par.
But beware – don't treat her with disdain
You invite the wrath of a woman's scorn,
When the wind gets up with the turning tide
Your score becomes like you – forlorn.

You now can't reach with two full woods
Where you once played a drive and wedge,
With the wind that's blowing from the south
You've played three shots to reach the edge.
So don't be fooled by the wide fairways
The verdant greens and the tight fescue,
These links will test the finest players
Just ask Jack Nicholas if it's true.

A Memory

MICHAEL BREED

It was a cold December evening, in fact Christmas Eve, as 14-year-old Luke was anxiously awaiting daybreak in his bed. His belief in Santa Claus had left a few years earlier, but still there was something mystical and magical about this night. This one night every year. The anticipation was overwhelming.

He had recently been introduced to golf two years prior when he broke his ankle in a basketball game. Not sure how to feed his athletic hunger, his father took him to a driving range 30 minutes from his house. Luke insisted to his dad that he had no interest in going and begrudgingly got into the 1966 red Mustang convertible. 'Just give it a try', his father begged, but it was more the car that convinced him to get in.

His father had arranged for William Lovelady, a local golf legend, to meet them at the range. Big Bill was how he was known and for good reason. See Bill was a beautiful golfer with a long effortless motion that was as natural as water flowing down a stream. He could hit a golf ball farther than you could see and was able to hit any shot on command. He had massive hands that looked like God made them for the purpose of holding a golf club. There was never any tension visible in Big Bill's hands nor any other part of his body.

When they arrived at the range, Big Bill greeted Luke with a smile and a powerful handshake. With a look of concern, he asked Luke about his ankle. 'A few more weeks in this cast and then I can run again', Luke proudly announced. 'When I finish with you today you might not need to run', Bill said with a gleam.

Forty-five minutes later, Luke was hitting the golf ball with ease: the kind you see from someone with way more experience than a first-timer. Luke's swing was simple and remarkably powerful with a grace that reminded Bill of Fred Couples. 'That's all for today', Big Bill announced. 'Work on what I have taught you and we'll do it again in a month.' Luke's shoulders sagged. 'That's it', he questioned. 'No, that's not it. It's just all for today', Bill responded.

Luke didn't want to leave. Though his hands hurt, he continued to practise. Working on the points that Big Bill had stressed, he continued to see success. Finally, his father said, 'We have to go home. Mom's making dinner and we've been here for four hours'. Luke couldn't believe it. He had become completely unaware of the time or the pain in his hands and in his ankle.

Reluctantly, he got into the Mustang, and they headed home. The 30-minute ride was full of questions from Luke to his dad. The final one he asked was, 'When can we do it again?' A smile came to his father's face. He asked Luke, 'Do you like golf?' 'I love it!', Luke replied.

Luke and had fallen in love with the sport. The challenge of athletic motion had always been something that fascinated him. But with golf there was something more. He would eventually see the golf course and its unimaginable beauty. The peacefulness he discovered was unparalleled yet there was a greater attraction. The chance to be with his father. To communicate about the challenges of the game and the challenges of life. The quiet moments of thought and reflection from the wisdom of his idol. The conversations of what was and what will be.

The game had hooked him but for more than the score he shot.

The thought required to improve. The effort to develop the needed skills for improvement. The mental fortitude to overcome doubt, fear and obstacles that were present in every round. He loved it and it was in his soul.

Finally, the sun had broken through on a crisp clear Christmas morning. Luke got of bed, opened his bedroom door, and proceeded to walk down the stairs. He could see the lights of the Christmas tree already turned on and he knew he was not alone. As he walked into the living room – the cast removed from his ankle months ago – he saw his father with a cup of coffee in his hands. The smile on his father's face was the hint he was looking for. Against the fireplace, arranged in perfect order, was a brand-new set of Titleist irons. It was exactly what he had hoped for. It was exactly what kept him awake all night. They were even more beautiful than he had imagined. Luke held each club, one at a time, with the grip Big Bill had taught him that day at the range, two years ago. As he put the last of the irons down, with tears in his eyes, he looked at his father. No words needed to be said. But he did. 'I love you dad. Thank you for everything.'

The Arnie Piece

JIM NUGENT

The year was 1975, and the good Jesuits at Loyola Academy in suburban Chicago saw fit to award me a diploma and send me off into the real world. My reward from my parents was a ticket to the US Open, being played at nearby Medinah Country Club shortly after graduation.

Jim Nugent

Medinah No. 3, one of three courses on an expansive piece of property, was a rumour to me. It had the reputation of being a beast. It was arguably the toughest and most famous of all the golf courses in the Chicagoland area. I had only read and heard about it. The course might as well have been 1,000 miles away, as I had never seen it. I couldn't wait to learn what the praise was all about.

I had, however, another, more urgent, matter at hand. I was going to see my very first golf hero, Arnold Palmer, play in the US Open.

Arnold, in the flesh. I could not contain my excitement.

Upon my arrival, I grabbed my pairing sheet and tried to figure out where the great man was. A glance at the leaderboard froze me: early in the first round, he was in red numbers! I made my way through the dense tree forests that defined Medinah No. 3 back in the day, eventually catching up to him.

Despite a field that had many of the greats, including Jack Nicklaus, Ben Crenshaw, Johnny Miller and Tom Watson, Palmer had the biggest gallery. His 'Army' cheered every shot, moaned at every missed putt, and revelled in the shared camaraderie of being with our hero as he competed in what he labelled 'the National Open'.

Palmer would shoot 69 that day, 2-under par, and he would go on to post a 6-over-par 290 and finish T9, three shots behind the champion, Lou Graham. It would be Palmer's final top-10 finish in the US Open and his second-to-last top ten in any major.

And to think I saw it with my own eyes.

Blairgowrie

ANN MACLAREN

At the beginning of the Second World War, when children from cities all over the UK were being evacuated to the countryside, my mother and her two younger brothers found themselves in Blairgowrie. It was their first time out of 'the Garngad' as it was then called – an area in the north-east of Glasgow, in the shadow of the St Rollox Locomotive Works.

They were all lodged in the Rosemount area of the town: Margaret who was nine years old, was given a home by a childless couple in the town. William, seven, and John, six, were sent to the home of an elderly lawyer, a kind and gentlemanly bachelor, who lived in a large house just along the road, opposite the golf course.

On their first morning, the boys went out to explore their new surroundings and found a beautiful expanse of well-cut grass awaiting them. They had never seen a golf course – not even in pictures – so they didn't know what it was. They assumed it was a park, like the Glasgow parks they had occasionally visited.

As they were walking across the grass, John found a wee white ball, then another, and another; then William found a couple. It's not clear why there were so many balls lying around on that particular morning, or why nobody was playing on the course; but in no time at all the boys' pockets were full and they had more balls stuffed down their jumpers. They decided they'd go back to the house and find a bag to put them in, then they'd go back and look for more. As they left the golf course, they saw

Margaret, who had come to see if her wee brothers were settling in. They excitedly showed her their stash. Margaret didn't know any more about golf than the boys did, so she didn't know what these balls were, but some kind of sixth sense told her they might just belong to somebody. She told the boys she wouldn't let them collect more until they'd asked their new guardian about them.

The lawyer was horrified when he saw all the stolen golf balls. He could have been incredibly angry and might have wondered what he'd let himself in for – giving a home to these boys whose background he knew very little about. He was, however, a kind and considerate man. He quietly explained a little about golf, and why it might be dangerous to walk across the course while a game was in play, and why these balls all belonged to someone who had paid for them. At no time did he mention the word stealing. He said he would take care of the return of the balls to the golf club, and they were sent back out to play. (They learned later that the lawyer had not taken the golf balls back to the club, because he didn't want the boys to be branded as trouble on their first day in town. Instead, he had gone out late at night and tipped them over the hedge at a spot where they would be easily seen.)

John and William were grateful that they had suffered no punishment that day for what, they later know, was theft. They had reckoned without Margaret, though, who took advantage of her superiority in age to give them both a good hard clip round the ear, which she knew, was exactly what their mother would have done.

Henry

JIM MACKINTOSH

There we were in the berry shade of a Perthshire
    summer,
You in a tumbleweed ball of grizzled golfing knowledge
And me, a nobody of nothing more than plooky bravado
Daring to wedge itself between the Lady Captain and You

Or somehow, that's how I have coloured time with rose
Tinted memories of Sanders, crimplened and coiffured
In faux tartan slacks wafting on to the eighteenth green
Measuring the distance to glory in his then familiar way,

Majors lost by inches still fresh yet not missed on that day.
Our memories fade sweetly, twist in the telling and now
I return to this one fifty years down the moonlit cart path
Reminiscing of Junior days at Blairgowrie, bravado now
    spent

Me still wedged between lavender cashmere and legend
Fraudulent and tense as I inhale your clipped gravel
    tones
Whispered into a giant bratwurst like boom
    microphone. You:
Henry Longhurst, tweed weft hunkered assurance in
    every word.

After the circus left, normality returned, mandatory
   junior medals
On the Wee Nine, the odd proffered foray on to the
   Rosemount
Where the approach to the eighteenth took on new
   meaning
No matter the score because Henry's voice now guided
   me in.

You still had the right words, still knew when silence was
   power
Still polishing the ordinary, still bejewelling occasional
   brilliance
on the manicured fringe of dreams, of sinking the glory
   putt.
I listen now and again for your silence, no longer
   counting the score.

THE BEST OF HENRY LONGHURST
Compiled and Edited by
Mark Wilson and Ken Bowden

'reminds us sadly that the old purple-faced
whisperer has gone but, joyfully, that
his old purple prose will live for as long as
literate men love games.'
Frank Keating THE GUARDIAN

Memories of Musselburgh

MUNGO PARK

Musselburgh holds a special place in the history of golf. Set within the racecourse, Musselburgh's 9-hole course was the home of the first Open Champion, Willie Park Snr, and four others. Between them they won the Championship eleven times.

I have three early memories of the town, one golfing, one celebratory and the third gastronomic. The first is of walking on the links, at a young age, with my grandfather, Mungo Park Jnr. He was a good-natured old man, who fed us pan drops as we walked. He would tell us tales of his father, who could (and did) drive a golf ball over the factory chimney that used to be at the west end of the Musselburgh Links and who would challenge others to play for money, sometimes giving himself a handicap by teeing off at every hole from the face of a pocket-watch. At that age, about five or six, I was aware that my grandfather and his father before him had played a bit of golf. It was very much later, when I started to undertake family research, that I realised how significant that 'bit of golf' had been – but more of that later.

The second of my Musselburgh memories I can date more precisely. It is of being hoisted onto the shoulders of the Champion at the Riding of the Marches in 1956. I think my father had been at Musselburgh Grammar School with him. I have a memory of him wearing armour and riding a horse, but it is more than likely that my subsequent childhood embellished this detail for better effect in the re-telling.

The third memory is gastronomic. It is of sitting on the work bench in Jimmy Stagg's saddlers' shop (Jimmy was my father's cousin, the son of Old Willie's sister, Euphemia), on the corner of Newbigging and the High Street with a Luca's ice cream cornet in my hand, surrounded by interesting shapes of leather, saddlery tools and golf bags that were waiting to be made or repaired. I was very young, and it was a magical place, with an intoxicating smell unlike any other.

My great grandfather, Willie Park Snr, was the son of a ploughman, James Park. Willie rose from the ranks of agricultural labourers and caddies to attain a level of golfing excellence that only 86 other golfers have reached in the years since, to be the Champion Golfer of the Year, The Open Champion.

Willie was astute enough to make the most of his golfing ability and to set up a flourishing ball and club-making business in Musselburgh. Golf quickly became the Park family trade, with three other brothers, Archie, Mungo and Davie using Musselburgh's leading position in the world of golf in the mid-nineteenth century to change the course of their lives. Four of Old Willie's sons also took to the business and the playing side of golf with flair. They, along with other Musselburgh families, fuelled the golf boom at the turn of the nineteenth and twentieth centuries. They led the export of the game to North and South America. As a result, my father, Jack Park, a doctor as well as a scratch golfer, was born and christened in Argentina, where in 1904 my grandfather (the kindly old man who in his later years fed me pan drops as we walked on the Links) won the first Argentine Open Championship.

He built a number of early courses in Argentina and North America, as did his brother Jack, working as jobbing professionals, teachers, designers, constructors and green-keepers. However far they went, the Parks retained their allegiance to Musselburgh, where they returned frequently. Young Willie, my great-uncle, who was the most extraordinary and enterprising member of the family, returned to Musselburgh from America when his health began to fail. My grandfather and grandmother (the first Argentine ladies champion) also spent their later years in Levenhall at the east end of the Links before my grandfather moved to Haddington to live with my aunt, Kay Ritchie, herself one of the five Park women to play golf for Scotland. The Parks' lives were bound up with golf, and with Musselburgh, first and last.

Appropriately, two members of the family were also the first and the last Open Champions to win at Musselburgh. Between 1874 and 1889, The Open was played over Musselburgh Links six times. In 1874, Old Mungo Park (old Willie's brother) won the first Open played there, and his nephew, Young Willie, took the prize in 1889 after a play-off against Andrew Kirkaldy.

Musselburgh has always had an important significance in the history and development of golf. It was to Musselburgh that the Edinburgh golfers resorted when overcrowding and the poor air quality of 'Auld Reekie' (Edinburgh) drove them out. They arrived in large numbers once the most important clubs moved there. Musselburgh, an industrial centre already, turned its industry to the making of new kinds of clubs and balls, transforming the game.

This year, the 150th playing of The Open will be held at St Andrews, which came to prominence after Musselburgh, eventually overtaking it in quality and popularity towards the end of the nineteenth century. It will be a celebration of an outstanding golfing spectacle that has delighted millions of people over its 150 years of play. The Open has come a long way since eight caddies from invited locations played for the first

Championship trophy, a Morocco leather belt decorated with ornate silver buckles in 1860. Although we will not be here to see it, I hope that in another 50 years, as they celebrate the 200th Open, future generations are able to enjoy the event as much as we do, and to do so in peace in a world that has finally learnt to overcome the madness of war, and the worst effects of a changing climate.

Musselburgh 1566

FINOLA SCOTT

Grand day tae be oot aboot,
but ower thrangit, aw the folk
haen a dauner by the watter.
Ilka body's here. Hiv yi heard?
the blether noo aboot the queen?
Mary an hir pals stoatin alang
the Links playin golf, agin.

Dinnae unnerstaund it masel.
Duntin a wee baw tae mak it fa
doon a wee hole. They say
she luves it. Ain o the things
she brung oer frae France.
Aye they dae it there an aw.
She stoats aboot in fancy clathes

Hir ladies hump hir sticks.
She cries thim cadets or mebbe
It's caddies, French onywey.
She's sae shair o hirsel she gembles
tae pruive she's the best o thim aw.
She brags she'll hae un trou en un.
Is Queen o Scotia nae eneuch?

Hard tae believe eh?

A Link with Peter and Alice Dye

BILLY DETTLAFF

I have learnt from my nearly 70 years in the game of golf that we golfers are more interrelated than we might imagine. This aspect helps make golf a memory maker. Think about your best round ever. *Who did you play with that day?* How about the professional tournaments you attended as a youngster or those in more recent years? *What was the most remarkable shot you witnessed in person? Who hit that shot?*

My golf story began with my father. He came to the game in 1907 as a nine-year-old caddie. He progressed through the caddie ranks over the next decade becoming proficient with a club in his hand. As a working-class 23-year-old veteran of World War I, he won a golf match to become the first golf professional at the new municipal golf course in Oshkosh, Wisconsin. That was in 1921.

Over the next 35 years, he dedicated his career to bringing local citizens into the game, first over the original 9-hole course, then in the mid-1930s, he led the expansion to 18-holes during the Great Depression. Funding came from President Roosevelt and the Works Progress Administration. That project allowed him to try his hand at golf course design. His design employed 'Golden Age of Golf Course Architecture' aspects such as chocolate drops, square greens, a punchbowl green and various bunker styles to add interest to the 92-acre municipal layout.

During his tenure, he made sure hundreds of young boys

had a chance to follow his path to the game through a caddie programme. His most famous protégé was Johnny Revolta. Johnny knew nothing about golf when he came to the golf course as a 12-year-old. Starting in 1923, he progressed quickly under my father's tutelage, winning the Wisconsin Caddie Championship two years later. Over the next couple of years, he was promoted to Caddie Master, then became one of my father's assistant professionals.

By the early 1930s, Johnny had risen through several head professional positions. He had also polished a great competitive game for such a young man. In 1935, Johnny had climbed to the top as leading money winner on the PGA Tour and a member of the Ryder Cup team. That season he won the Western Open, a Major of the time, and the PGA Championship, still a Major today, by defeating Tommy Armour 5&4 in match play. After retiring from the PGA Tour for family life, Johnny earned recognition as one of America's premier golf teachers. He was the featured instructor on golf's first ever TV show broadcast in Chicago. His top-selling instruction book included a dedication to my father.

Fast forward to 2010 and the 75th Anniversary of Johnny's PGA Championship. The tournament was in Wisconsin at Whistling Straits. Johnny remained Wisconsin's only PGA Champion. I was pleased to write an article on Johnny's accomplishment and career for the PGA Championship program.

I returned home to Wisconsin to attend the Championship. Standing outside the stone clubhouse on a beautiful sunny afternoon, I ran into Pete Dye, the Hall of Fame golf course architect of name for Whistling Straits, as well as TPC Sawgrass, from which I had recently retired. We had gotten to know each other a few years earlier during his renovation work on the

L-R: Billy Dettlaff and the late Pete Dye at TPC Sawgrass in 2007

TPC Sawgrass Stadium Course. I was excited to tell him about the article I had written on Johnny Revolta and to share my father's influence on the young Johnny.

Pete looked at me, astonished. *Your father taught Revolta?* Revolta was Alice's teacher! In her youth, Pete's wife, Alice, was a leading women's amateur player and later won back-to-back USGA Women's Senior Amateur titles in 1978 and 1979. Before they were married in 1950, she was Alice Holliday O'Neal. She eventually collected nine Indiana women's amateur titles. Alice was proudly featured in Revolta's book, *Short Cuts to Better Golf*.

I hadn't previously linked the names of O'Neal and Dye and only then had the full story. Pete credited Johnny's teaching for Alice's success. Learning this, I thought my father would have been proud of his extended influence in the game.

Early in their golf course construction careers, Pete and Alice made an extensive visit to Scotland to better understand the history and philosophy of golf design. One of their most influential visits was to Prestwick Golf Club on Scotland's west coast. Particularly impactful was the 3rd hole – 'The Cardinal Hole' – which features a broad and extensive use of railroad ties. Wooden embankments such as those at Prestwick became a Dye design signature throughout his career.

And so, I realised golf is so much more than a game. Playing, watching and reading about golf links us to millions of fellow golfers worldwide. We each share our own memories from the game, yet somehow, we are all interrelated. Don't ever hesitate to share your memories. You never know how uniquely you might be linked to the person you are speaking with!

Extracts from Dreams of Scottish Youth

GRAHAM FULTON

On quiet days with no one around I play putting inside the house. I open the sliding doors and set up the little metal mobile putting hole in a far corner of the dining room and pick a spot, a specific part of the carpet pattern at the opposite corner of the living room, to act as a putt-off point. I choose about 50 names and type them out in no apparent order on a couple of sheets of paper. The famous and not so famous golf names of the day. Tony Jacklin, Lee Trevino, Gary Player. I take a shot for each, then, once they've all had one, type up the leader board in the correct order then do it all again. The typing takes longer than the playing. I like the procedure of making a list. My own random favourites start to emerge, and I probably try a bit harder with them. I try not to show favouritism, but it happens. If a shot goes wild and ends up under a chair, then that player is doomed. It could be four shots instead of one or two. There's no way back. I do this for a few rounds then it fizzles out. Unfinished. The summer is too long. Time is too short.

'I Hear You Knocking' by Dave Edmunds is number one. It's quite good but seems to be on all the time. Sick of it. I get Arnold Palmer's Pro Shot Golf for Christmas. A golf club contraption with a small version of Arnold Palmer at the bottom holding a very small club. Unsmiling face and neat hair. A lever to pull to make him swing. You try and land the ball on a spongy green that won't stay flat in the middle of the carpet. You can change clubs if required. This is what Christmas is all about. On Boxing

Day, you play with it a little bit less and even less on the day after. After a reasonable while it's put into a cupboard. You sometimes catch a glimpse in the future of his blank plastic head, accusing eyes, when you're rummaging around looking for something else.

Our college year and the one above us goes for a week to a children's home near Turnberry for some reason. A change of scenery for the chumps. The girls get to stay in a nice house with real bedrooms, but the bad boys must sleep in a dormitory-style barracks on thick and crinkly incontinence sheets. People fart when the lights go out. A bit like a borstal or an asylum. There's a window right next to the breakfast table and a wee dog appears each morning to look at us eating and get some s craps. We call him Cracker Dug after Sandy says, 'See that wee dug, he's a wee cracker that dug'. We take turns at washing dishes. When we have spare time, we wander across The Open Championship golf course and buy a carry-out and a jar of pickled onions and get pissed in a bunker as we sing 'Oh Bondage! Up Yours!'

The Victory

ROSS KILVINGTON

26 May 2017 is a day etched permanently into my mind and regardless of what happens in the future, it's not one I'm ever likely to forget. Why? It was the first time I managed to get the better of my dad at the greatest game ever invented.

It only took 16 years to happen mind you, but it was worth the wait. To people who don't play golf, or any sport, it doesn't sound like a momentous occasion, but to me it was everything. Every single time we played a round I was desperate to finally triumph, only to be let down by a poor shot here and there over the last few holes, which my dad punished.

Teeing up on the 18th was always the worst, especially knowing that barring a major collapse, I wouldn't be able to prevail, and the final putts were always met with a 'good game, there's always next time, eh?'

For those that play the sport, sometimes it isn't about competition, the sheer will to win and defeat all that cross our paths, other things are perhaps more important. Things such as companionship or the chance to spend three to four hours bonding over a shared love of the game. Even trivial things such as conversations can be replaced by the odd 'good shot' or 'nice putt' and the sound of your own heartbeat as you line up a crucial putt.

My dad used to play golf a lot when he was younger, but due to the nature of his life and the ever-increasing demands of work and parenthood, he stopped for quite a while. The turning point came around 2001. I can vividly recall watching, with him,

David Duvall win The Open and decided that I fancied doing a bit of that, hitting a wee ball with a metal stick, it all seemed fairly straightforward. Of course, that meant he had to show me the ropes.

The innocence of youth, eh? Turns out it was just slightly more complex than that! My dad went and bought a new driver that summer and took me out to the driving range for my first shot at playing a game which would – and still does – perplex me every time I play.

I caught the bug, and we would go out to the range whenever time allowed, but it wasn't until I was 13 that I was let loose on the actual course. My parents basically moved next door to Dunnikier Park Golf Course, which was fantastic as it meant I could sneak on early in the morning or late at night to practise as much as I wanted.

Naturally, the first few times playing over 18 holes were tough, but I soon got the hang of it and was challenging my pals before long. The summer saw endless days spent on the course, winning, and losing aplenty whilst consuming everything I could which would help me play better.

Time marched on and still no victory over my dad, I blamed it on experience (a perfect excuse) but in reality, my dad had excellent temperament. He was more of the Bjorn Borg style – cool, calm and a bad shot didn't get the better of him – add into that 'Hoganesque' accuracy and you could see what I was up against. Whereas I was more akin to John McEnroe – rebel, temperamental and complained, a lot.

Golf was eventually put on the back burner as I finished school and went to university. I didn't play much, if at all for around four to five years as the game slipped to the back of my list of priorities.

Then, in October 2014, my dad asked if I fancied a round, out of the blue. I couldn't recall the last time I picked up a golf club never mind hit a shot and I responded like a whippet; it was on!

The outcome didn't change, victory for the elder Kilvington sent me home with a renewed focus on the game. I knew if I practised, then my time would come.

Fast forward two and a half years and I was ready. We began playing every Friday evening as the summer loomed on the horizon and even though the first few matches ended in defeat, I was getting better and striking the ball as well as ever.

That day, 26 May, had a different feel to it that I still cannot describe. The weather was great, I had practised well all week and I just felt confident this was going to be the day that the victory would be mine.

The funny thing is, I still can't remember what the final score was or the vast majority of my shots, which is unusual as I always pick out one or two that I think back on and try to replicate for future rounds. Perhaps I was in the zone and focussing too much on one shot at a time to really remember what went well and what didn't.

It felt like a watershed moment. We have traded blows back and forth since that Friday evening, but nothing will come close to the feeling I got when walking down the 18th, knowing what had eluded me for 16 years was in my grasp.

It is a momentous day when you get the better of someone who has taught you how to play a sport or a game. It's like a rite of passage. Once it occurs, things can never be the same again.

As I write this, I recall the last time me and my dad played a round. It was July 2020, just as everyone felt like life was slowly returning to normal following the Covid lockdown (how wrong we were) and whilst both of us were on furlough, it seemed like the perfect opportunity.

The rustiness affected me more than him (I'm convinced he had been out sneaking in nine holes here and there) and he took me to the cleaners!

It's fast approaching two years since then and I desperately want revenge, but like my dad before me, there is a stage in life where other things take precedence, such as family and work. I reckon my clubs thank me as they hold a permanent residence in the garage, far away from the wild swings and the constant neglect they receive out on the course.

Golf is a wonderful game, maybe the best of games and one that I love and despise in equal measure. The pandemic has taught me to never take anything for granted and hopefully this attitude continues when I take to the course again with my dad.

Only if I win, of course.

The Gowf Experience

SHEILA TEMPLETON

I wis nineteen year auld an gan oot wi a lad
afa keen oan the gowf. Sae fan he prigged
tae teach me the airts o the ancient game
– fit cud I say? I wis fair teen wi the noshun.

Hazleheid 9-hole course in Aiberdeen
an a bonnie day. Fit cwid ging wrang?

Ye dinna ken a chiel's hert ontil ye've lat him
gie ye the finer pynts of the hale business
– takkin yer stance, far tae place yer fingers
lattin go inta the swing Keep yer ee oan the ba!
Ach ye're nae listenin. Jist waatch me a mintie.

Sae it winna surprise tae kythe that half-wyes roon,
ma mood hud dairkened – an I made up ma myn
tae sprint aheed o him, get the wee fite tee stuck in
– an lat swing – lang afore he'd reach me.

But fit is it they say? Lat God ken yer plans
so she can hae a gweed laach?

I peched oan tae the 6th tee, stuck it in the grun
swung the No 5-iron he'd lent me – wi muckle virr
– but the ba steyed still, as the club flichered up
richt inta the lift – disappeared amang the brinches
o a muckle great oak tree. Niver tae be seen again.

Oh we lookit an poked an tried tae sclim up
but nae eiss. Cam back fan winter frosts
hud killed the leaves — shairly we'd see it.

But we niver did. A muckle begeck. That No 5-iron
as lost tae the warld as oor buddin romance.

Tiger

HUGH MACDONALD

There are two homes of golf. The first, and most illustrious, hosts the 150th Open championship. The other hosts only my memories, and once, a long time ago, my dreams.

St Andrews needs no ring walk, no rousing music, no dramatic prose. It sits by the water and accepts its due quietly and with no little dignity.

Even during Open week, in the glare of the world's media, it holds secrets. In 2005, in search of a story, I rose before the sun and made my way along the coastal path to the course.

It was well known that Tiger Woods practised early. But where and when to trap him?

The where seems obvious. But there was a twist. The when was vague but the answer was emphatically, 'very early'.

Just after 4am, I was standing behind the first tee at the Old Course on a practice day. Peering into the gloom with a determined focus, I kept a lookout for Tiger while engaging in conversation with a Geordie security man on the great Scots who had played with Newcastle United.

Gently, but generously, he made my day. 'If I was looking for Tiger, I would not be standing here', he said. 'I would be on the second tee.' He had imparted the secret.

I rushed over the lush fairway and, when the whin parted, there stood Tiger, having walked straight from his hotel on to the course and having, presumably, decided that the first hole need not be negotiated for fear of arousing the interest of early birds.

The following hours provided an extraordinary lesson in golfing prowess and the demands of fame.

Tiger could be appreciated on the telly. My knowledge of the intricacies of golf was (and is) non-existent. His masterpieces could be seen by me in the broadest of strokes. But, on that beautiful morning in Fife, I was exposed to greatness in all its detailed glory.

Tiger was trying the course on for size. It fitted like a Saville Row suit. Falling in behind his entourage and that of his playing partner, I was immediately aware of certain truths. The first was that Tiger was the king of this jungle. His every remark was greeted by the sort of laughter afforded a revolutionary leader who has a working and red-stained guillotine.

His golfing skill was obvious even to one crudely schooled in the sport. As the light played along the fairways, it was possible to look up and follow the shape of his shots. They rested where he ordered them to lie. And on one occasion when a shot mischievously broke ranks and nestled in a bush, Tiger merely saw this as an opportunity to demonstrate a physical strength to accompany his innate talent.

In the gaggle of holes around the turn, his ball disappeared so far into a mass of green and a clutch of tendrils. It was a bush in the same way that Everest is a hill.

Hardly breaking stride, Tiger wielded his club in the manner of William Wallace bumping into an English knight. One dramatic swish and the ball was deposited on the green.

It was impossible not to gasp. Tiger chortled. It was difficult to discern if his amusement was piqued by the brutal beauty of the shot or the reaction it had evoked in mere mortals. Perhaps both.

It was evident, though, that the deed had been done many times in many places. It was not a matter for exultation for Tiger, rather one of expectation.

The other certainty occurred gradually. As a mild almost half-hearted haar cleared, it was obvious that a crowd had gathered. As Tiger's round stretched towards 8am, there was a gallery. It was respectful but appreciative. His shots were cheered, his every step was greeted with cries of support.

Tiger Woods on 18th at St Andrews

The Tiger smiled but one could not quite discern what he was feeling. In truth, no one ever could. He just walked and hit or hit and walked with immaculately white balls arcing unfailingly towards pins like heat-seeking missiles discovering a minute patch of lava.

The show was becoming ever more public. The crowds were increasing as word of mouth became roar of mouth and it seemed most people in Fife had not only heard that Tiger was on the course but were determined to join him.

It was then that the greatest golfer of his age took an early bow. His round petered out on the back nine. Enough had been seen. Enough had been done. A game had been tweaked and perhaps even a plan had been formulated.

Swiftly but decorously, aided by the sort of security that would surround afternoon tea between the Pope and the President, he disappeared into the whin, leaving only the memory of having witnessed greatness at close quarters in dawn's early light.

The other home of golf is harder to define. It is individual. It is where one first sclaffed the first ball and strangely and immediately became in thrall to the most infuriating of games.

It was Linn Park for me. We called it bandit country and not because of the bare-faced, straight-hitting lies of handicappers who claimed double figures but played in singles.

Linn Park, a half a century ago, was best approached warily. Its boundaries tickled the surrounding badlands of Glasgow south of the river. The hazards were not confined to patches of sand or thickets of green. There was the par-five where one of the party was posted on a hill to ensure all drives over it were not carried away by enterprising ball boys. There were moments when one carried a 5-iron in the manner of John Wayne on the sands of Iwo Jima.

But it is where I first played golf. My introduction was brusque. My father was a collector of anything. In the days before eBay (in truth these were the days before mostly anything), he picked up a set of clubs, possibly from a house clearance.

The bag was solid if well used. The clubs were adequate, certainly for a novice. I called my mates and we headed to Linn Park. They had an assortment of clubs that stuck out from the bag like a hastily assembled consignment of large lollipops.

We lugged them on the bus, decanted at Netherlee and then walked up to Linn Park to take our place in the queue.

We were members of a crowd that giggled while not quaking in apprehension. Every tee shot on the first hole was viewed by a crowd so large that it would put the Ryder Cup to shame. Many cracked before its eyes.

One's amusement at the fecklessness of the Setterday morning golfer was tempered by the immediate realisation that one was up next and that one did not do impersonations of Tom Watson or, indeed, any Watson who could hit a straight drive.

My most glorious moment, which my friends say they will forget soon, occurred in the early 1970s when my drive hit a tree on my left and rolled conveniently but humiliatingly back to my feet.

The round thus under way we galloped and gasped around Linn Park. There was the imperative not to hold up anyone behind. One didn't play through at Linn Park but over and on in the manner of a runaway tank. Slow play could bring a tee shot down on one's head. It was best to be brisk.

We loved it though. The shots piled up in number and, occasionally, in quality. I cannot be certain at this moment where my car keys are. I can recall in exquisite detail a 7-iron that soared like a Mickelson missile and plopped perfectly into the hole. I could not have been happier if I had meant it.

We kept coming back until we didn't. Weans, work, more weans and more work, intervened and golf became a casualty.

My interaction with the game was to witter and wander, that is to visit big tournaments, watch the greats and try to record what I had seen and what it might mean.

It is how the road stretched from Linn Park to St Andrews. It is why the hacker on the South Side of Glasgow became the observer in a famous corner in Fife.

It is why that Tiger laugh on a morning in 2005 has lingered with me over the years. He went on to win that Open with an ease that suggested if the tournament had lasted another few holes, he would have lapped the field.

It brought a Claret Jug and a beaming smile. But the great golfer has had his pain, his shame and his descent. But so have we all.

However, there is redemption even consolation in the most unlikely of spots. I wonder if he remembers the fun he had on the course on a perfect Tuesday. I do.

It's a Breeze

ROY MACKENZIE

Breezy wind behind
Swing easy
Head down, eye on the ball
You're on the dance floor

Par 3's are birdie chances
Par 4's the ditches are in play
Par 5's are still long
it's fun today

Then into the wind's teeth
A 3-club change
Foundations and relax
Visualise, visualise, visualise

Focus wavers as body tires
Stay in the present and in process
Don't worry about others
Concentrate, concentrate, concentrate

Reiss Links

When the Chips are Down

DIANE McKEE

I was brought up on golf, whether trailing around a golf course after my dad and older brothers or watching it on television. Back in the 1970s and 1980s, golf on television was mostly to be found in the form of popular entertainment programmes like the BBC's hugely popular *Pro-Celebrity Golf*. This paired celebrities up with professionals, including real characters of the game such as Greg Norman, Johnny Miller and Seve Ballesteros. The celebrities were a mixed bag: comedians such as Ronnie Corbett, actors including 007 himself, Sean Connery, and sportsmen such as footballer Kenny Dalglish. It was very light-hearted and gave the viewer a chance to see professional golfers in a different setting from the usual tournaments. *Around with Alliss*, another BBC programme, saw Peter Alliss, the famous commentator and former professional golfer, playing a round of golf with a famous person. He was perfect in this role, getting a wide variety of people – from Terry Wogan to Kiri Te Kanawa – to open up to him about their lives. The programme was a great success, running for six series.

The Open Championship was the highlight of the golfing year and I remember the excitement when we upgraded from a black and white television to a colour set. Suddenly the screen was filled with green, the players like little splodges of pastel and primary colours on the canvas. You could even see the ball take flight, a white dot against a sky most often grey but occasionally a brilliant blue. Favourite players in our house included Tom Watson, with his endearing smile and friendly demeanour, the swashbuckling Seve Ballesteros and, in particular, Lee Trevino. To a family somewhat vertically challenged, Trevino appealed partly because of his stature but also because of his big personality, someone who liked to engage with the fans. He was also fun to watch, taking chances and playing shots which other golfers would never have tried. He was famous for the 'bump and run', a technique he perfected on the dry golf courses in Texas, where he grew up. This was perfect for links golf.

My parents took me along with them as spectators to several Opens, mostly in Scotland. Carnoustie, Muirfield, Turnberry and Royal Troon were particularly memorable. Sometimes, we'd follow a particular group of players; at other times, we sat in one of the stands overlooking the greens, eating our sandwiches and drinking tea from flasks. It wasn't very glamorous, but it was a great day out, especially when waiting to see one of the big names arrive. I have two particular memories. One was seeing Anthea Redfern, the then wife of Bruce Forsyth and hostess on *The Generation Game*, in a Portakabin toilet out on the Carnoustie course in 1975 – great excitement to see a Saturday night TV personality in person! The other was in 1972 at Muirfield in East Lothian. To our great delight, Lee Trevino won The Open that year, beating England's Tony Jacklin. On the final day, we were stood near the 17th green and watched as Trevino chipped in, to resounding cheers from the crowd. It was a thrilling moment. Even my mother, a long-suffering golfing widow, was bowled over by it. Seeing 'wee Lee' chipping in and going on to win at Muirfield was a story which was often recounted in our family over the years, as golf continued to provide us with great stories and happy memories.

Gift

YVONNE GRAY

It was all green and all rough, the hidden field where I first learned to swing a golf club in a summer that is both recent and long ago. Two sides were lined by privet hedges that bordered the gardens of council houses in Wilson Avenue, the other two by high brick walls, and the overhanging branches of trees in the gardens of large houses on London Road and Holehouse Road. From my grandmother's garden, I could squeeze through the privet hedge where it met the end of the wall.

Most often, the field was empty. I would play on my own – an acrobat practising handstands, legs swung up again and again till at last my heels met the wall, or a horse that veered in circles, sweeping through clover and buttercups. I made feast platters – dockens laden with rowanberries, grass seed and fragments of chewed sourock balled into peas – careful offerings for the fairies that lived beneath the hedge. I searched for four-leaf clovers and was wildly excited when I found one, overwhelmed by a sense of magic, the luck it would bring. Most of all, I wanted to grow wings.

Sometimes, children appeared from the narrow lane at the top end of the field, or from other gardens, jumping from the wall or swinging down from low branches. A visitor, I would hang back on the edge of their games. Other times, I tied grass traps to trip the boys who played football, a competent and exclusive gang.

One evening, I drifted towards a small group of children who stood around an elderly man. He swung and hit a golf ball – a brisk thwack and it sang into the blue, arced and vanished into grass far down the field. He drew another from a pocket, positioned himself and swung again.

A gleam of light.

A sharp sigh as iron sliced air. Thwack.

Another ball. A sigh and a thwack.

One after another the balls soared and fell.

And when they had all gone, I joined the others and searched the grass at the bottom of the field. We collected them and ran back with them cupped in our hands like eggs. He took them and slid them, one at a time, into his pockets.

Mr Aitken. He was in his eighties – some 20 years older than my grandmother.

I made a friend my own age, Christine, and we often met and played in the field that summer. Sometimes Mr Aitken was there, and we would watch him practise and collect the balls he hit. One day he handed each of us an iron. He showed us how to interlock our hands and grasp the shaft. How to space our feet, matching the gap to our shoulders' width. We learned to drop our knees, arms, heads. To take a practice shot – rotate and raise the club back and up. To swing in an inverted arc, remembering to follow through, lifting our heads and eyes at last.

My club felt too long, and I slugged it hard into the ground, jarring my arms and wrists and loosening a divot behind the ball. Mr Aitken heeled the lump down. I adjusted my grip and swung again, topping the ball so it trickled forward a few inches.

I don't know how many evenings we spent this way: Mr Aitken patiently explaining the grip, the stance, the swing. Christine progressed more than me and one day he told her to keep the

6-iron she was using so she could practise on her own. It was a spare, he said. He had another at home.

I continued to swing and was pleased when the ball gained height and flew some distance in a low arc down the field. A new ball placed, I gathered myself, checking my shoulders, knees, feet. I tapped the ball gently, checking where to aim the club. I raised my arms, rotating my body, and swung through — effortlessly it seemed.

The iron gleamed and sliced the air with a sigh.

A crisp thwack, and the ball soared up and up above the treetops and sang into the blue. It arced down and vanished — where, I never knew.

That night, my grandmother and I were finishing our tea when the doorbell rang. Mr Aitken was on the front step, a 4-iron in his hands, a gift for me before I left.

I am now the age my grandmother was then.

I may have dreamed in that moment of being a champion golfer, sending balls into flight so they soared then dropped like gifts from the sky onto a distant green. I practised for some weeks — but never really followed through. I played a few holes with my father who took up golf himself, and later, with my sons who grew up and learned to play in Stromness on a course bounded by Hoy Sound where the current sweeps balls sliced out-of-bounds into Scapa Flow — or out into the Atlantic.

And yet I don't think these early swings in the hidden field were swiped into vacancy, or that the ball that vanished was ever truly lost.

Today, as I practise arm rotation at the piano, I sound, here and there, a chord that truly sings and draw the arc of a phrase that soars before its dying fall.

I have wings now, and at times I can fly.

Shanks for the Good Times

STEVE FINAN

The funniest thing I ever did see
Was on Carnoustie's 15th tee
The day my old beloved father
Was injured in a golf palaver.
Now I was just a callow youth
But that fine day I learned a truth
A lesson seared with irons hot —
Watch out when you play a shot.

My dad teed up to hit the thing
And I stood back to let him swing
His head held still, he struck his ball
The stars did cross and fates befall
His shank was headed far astray
But something hard was in the way
The drinking fountain by the tee
It's concrete base was hit, you see.
Dad found an angle quite acute
A rebound back to him did shoot
That ball with venom held within
It damn well hit him on the shin!
He roared, he cursed, he shouted hoarse
They heard him all around the course

The St Andrews Open, 19 July, 1946

He hopped, he danced, he ran amuck
(I think he mentioned Donald Duck).
His trouser cuff rolled up that leg
Revealed a lump shaped like an egg.
But no help came from me that day
I'd fallen down, near passed away
I laughed so hard I couldn't breathe
While he did rant, while he did seethe.
His pain wore off after a while
And dad eventually cracked a smile
We both agreed that that day's game
(Despite it making him quite lame)
Was one that would forever be
Recounted fondly, and with glee.
That sunny day is long since gone
And dad now plays his rounds upon
That great big golf course in the sky
Where every shot doth truly fly.
Dad plays there, 18 holes a day
I miss him more than I can say.
The best thing you can ever do
For someone who meant much to you.
Is think of them when at their best
All full of life and laughs and zest.
So still I grin when I recall
My old dad's fury at that ball.

Winnie Palmer, wife of Arnold Palmer, watching her husband at The Open 1965, Royal Birkdale

Quaint Customs and No Pints for Ladies

RONA FITZGERALD

Clontarf Golf Club, my club for almost 20 years, is situated between a main road and the railway on the north side of Dublin city. The course was and is a short 18-hole golf course but challenging because of narrow fairways and a tricky twelfth hole that includes a quarry.

Looking back on those years, lots of warm memories come to the fore: games played well or badly of course – golfers are famed for their detailed report of the game! In addition, I remember friendships, participation in everything from golf competitions to presentations, singing with friends at the Captain's dinner, my mother Eileen's satire on the club that she wrote and produced for years.

There were personalities and cranky folk, a span of ages from teens to eighties. It taught me how to relate to different people from all walks of life. In the last two years, many of us have experienced the loss of those connections that sports bring whether you are a participant or a spectator.

Moments that stand out include caddying for my mam and dad at a big competition in 1971 when I was 17. They were surprise winners of the semi-final, playing the final on the same day. My brother and I were so tired after 36 holes and had very little to eat that I began to fantasise about a plate of chips and a cup of tea in the clubhouse.

My strongest memory is of caddying for my friend, the late Therese Moran – later Therese O'Reilly. She was an international golfer and Irish champion. In the late 1970s, I caddied for her in Cork at an interprovincial tournament. She was a skilled golfer, a good friend and incredible fun. I am pleased to say she won her matches.

For me, golf has a long association. When I joined at 15, we were called juveniles. Lady golfers of all ages were banned from the snooker/pool room and were not allowed to consume pints of beer.

Golf is hard for young people, learning patience, getting the rhythm of the course which seemed long at first. Once you play regularly – which is no guarantee of being any good – you must learn to support your partner. Many a time, I was encouraged and guided around the course by a more established golfer who knew I was doing well. In later years, I reciprocated.

My early club set was a 3-wood from my grandfather who was six foot five. I was tall for a girl in those days at five eight, but it was a challenge. I also had my mam Eileen's 7-iron, a 4-iron and a putter she got for coupons during the Second World War. I got down to a handicap of 16 with those clubs.

I'm grateful for all that golf has given me though still perplexed at the 'no pool'– perhaps they thought it was unladylike – and the 'no pints'. Although not a pint drinker, it irked. They were happy for me to pay for pints for my brother and a friend but not to drink it!

A Song of Putting

W M LINDSAY
First published in *College Echoes*, XIII, 17 January 1902

O aa the strokes that's in the game
Which is your choice? Gie it a name,
The drive, say you; the loft, say you;
The brassy-shot, the cleek-shot – but
   Gie me the putt.
The wee bit pat, nae mair nor that,
The canny touch, scarcely saw much,
The stroke that sends the ballie in,
O that's the stroke to far you win!

Your 'far and sure's' a splendid motto,
When I was young' 'twas aa tho't o,
To swipe my fill, to hae my will,
To lace intil't wi flurry – but
   Gie me the putt,
The wee bit pat, nae mair nor that,
The canny touch, scarcely sae much.
The drive's but silver, solid gold
The stroke that sees the ballie holed.

I've watched them stan wi feet wide planted
An swing their club like men demented;
Then crack! An whew! Awa she flew,
The soarin, sounin rocket – but
   Gie me the putt,

Selection of very early putters

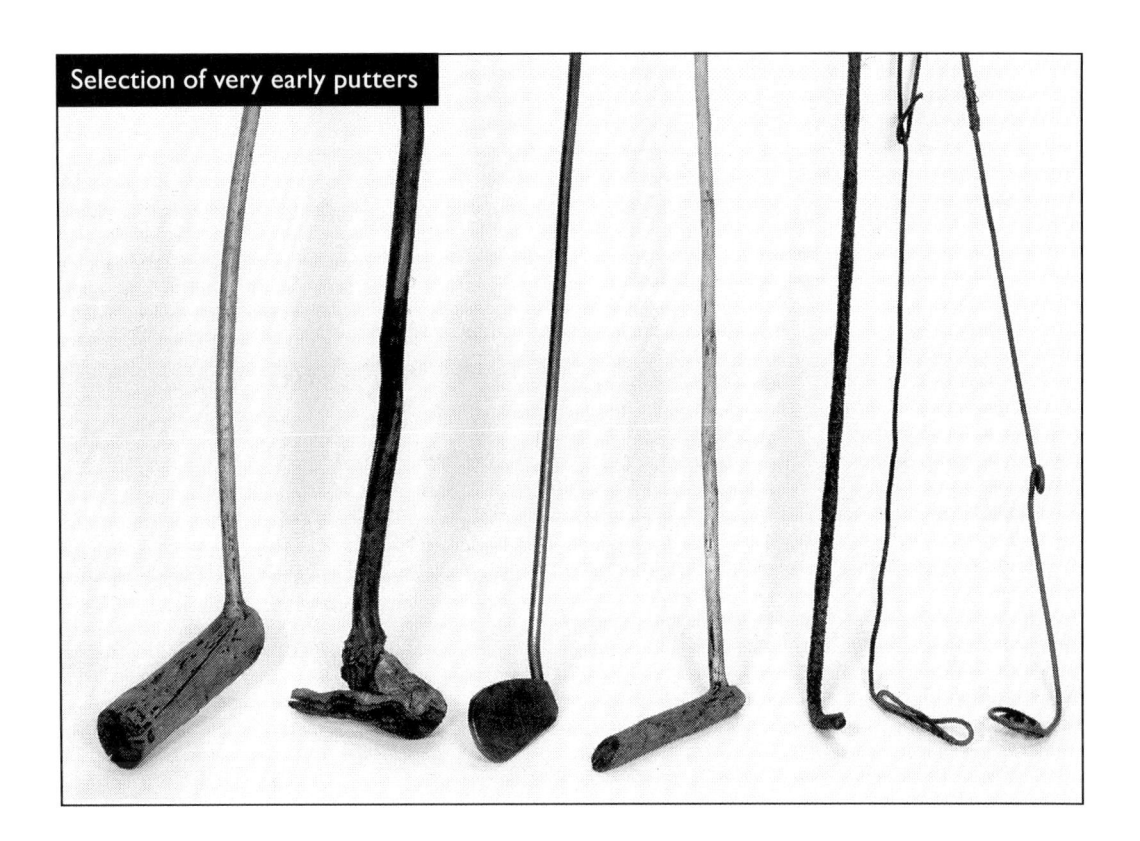

The wee bit pat, nae mair than that,
The canny touch, scarcely saw much,
Yon drive, the talk o half the toun,
It didna send the ballie doon.

On life's last green ane wish I'll utter:
'Leave to my han my faithful putter,
My steps to say on my lang way.
I fain wad tak nane ither but
   The club to putt
To gie the pat, nae mair not that,
The canny touch, scarcely saw much.
St Peter willna think it's in
To let my wee bit putter in.'

Golf in a Scottish Winter

COLIN MACLEAN

'You're mad', said my mum as I left the house on my bike with my half set of second-hand clubs on my back to cycle five miles to the golf course in the freezing rain. But she made sure there was a big pot of Scotch broth ready when I got home.

'You're mad', said my girlfriend when I suggested I take her for her first game of golf. We played two holes in freezing fog where you couldn't see anything you hit more than 30 yards. I gave in after two holes and we went for a coffee instead. That was her last game of golf. We've been married nearly 50 years and she still wins at crazy golf.

'You're mad', said the starter at Carnoustie when Tom and I turned up in February to play in sleet and a howling gale off the North Sea. We enjoyed our visit to the tea hut at the 10th hole that day! I played to my usual poor standard but got two off my handicap because the other mad souls played so much worse than usual that week.

'You're mad', said Ian when his caddy told him to drive 45 degrees right of the flag at the 8th hole on the Old Course. The gale brought his ball to within three feet of the hole, and he got a birdie.

'You're mad', said my daughter when I told her I only wear one glove when I play golf – however cold it is. 'You get a better feel of the club with your right hand if you don't wear a glove', I said. I didn't admit that my fingers freeze to the shaft, and I don't feel anything with my right hand from November to March.

'We're mad', we said to each other as we played on rock-hard

First tee at Burnside Course, Carnoustie

ground where every shot bounced off at random, our shoes had blocks of ice stuck to the bottom and putting on the winter greens was a complete lottery. We got back to the clubhouse to find George drinking a quiet coffee beside the heater. 'Lovely weather today. Where were you?', we asked.

'We're mad', we said to each other as we played in squelching mud after a week of rain. Balls didn't bounce, they disappeared into the mud as soon as they landed. We got back to the clubhouse to find George drinking a quiet coffee beside the heater. 'Lovely weather today. Where were you?', we asked.

'You're mad', I said as Arlene fired her low runner straight at a huge bunker. 'Nae bother', she said as the ball bounced on the frozen sand, out of the bunker, onto the green and ended up six inches from the cup.

'They're mad', we said about the young couple jogging past in their shorts and T-shirts as we stood on the tee wearing our six layers of thermal golf clothes.

You have to be mad to play in a Scottish winter, but on a sunny day, when the wind drops and you can see for miles in the crisp air, you get your reward. Friends for life, regular exercise and so much to laugh about and remember. Nothing like it.

Note: *Edinburgh U3A Golf Club. The U3A is an international network of local organisations that provide a wide variety of activities for mainly retired people. The Edinburgh golf section has over 50 members. Most of us play every week at the Wee Braids golf course in Edinburgh where we have our own handicapping system that takes account of our 'Blue Stakes Rule'; that you get a free drop if you land in a group of trees that are younger than you! The tales in this short story, and others, are shared in the coffee shop after our Monday round.*

Kingarrock Hickory Golf

DAN BARLOW

While the 'official' history of Kingarrock Hickory Golf Course might begin in the 1920s, I start this account with a much more ancient and illustrious connection to the game of golf. Kingarrock is situated on land now pertaining to Hill of Tarvit, a National Trust property just south of Cupar, yet the land was originally part of the much older estates of Wemysshall and Scotstarvit. It is no coincidence that the near neighbours, James Wemyss and David Scott of Scotstarvit, were both among the 22 'founding fathers' who in 1754 established the Society of St Andrews Golfers. The reader will know that this early golf club evolved into what we now know as the Royal & Ancient.

Kingarrock Hickory Golf Course occupies an idyllic setting in the hills of North East Fife, with stunning views down to the picturesque village of Ceres, yet its more modern-day origins lie in the dusty industrial world of the nineteenth-century jute mills of Dundee.

One Dundee mill owner, Frederick Shar, was in many ways the archetypal Victorian industrialist. Born into a family of relatively 'new money', but no doubt keen to enjoy the life hitherto reserved for a more aristocratic elite, he must have jumped at the chance to acquire a country estate a stone's throw from the railway station at Cupar within easy reach of his beloved Royal & Ancient, just ten miles away. And so, at the turn of the twentieth century the historic Wemyss Hall passed from being the ancient ancestral seat of the Wemyss family into being Hill of Tarvit, complete with its new modern house built to house Frederick's burgeoning collection of art and antiques. This was also to be a family home and we can imagine that on the gently undulating land later occupied by the golf course, Frederick's 10-year-old son, Hugh, spent his school holidays playing among those same ancient oak trees, ditches and dykes which today serve to enhance (or frustrate) the game played by visitors to Kingarrock.

It was not until the early 1920s that Hugh, having survived the horrors of the trenches, persuaded his amiable (and wealthy) father to turn the fields beyond the ha-ha into the 9-hole course we see today. No doubt a round of golf on the family course was most restorative for Hugh after what he must have witnessed just a few years earlier.

Kingarrock Hickory Course

The course back then must have looked much as it does now as still today the groundsman is assisted by his team of woolly four-legged helpers who graze the rough and fairways of the course, thereby helping to maintain the slightly wilder look of a 1920s course.

It was certainly intended as a family course, evidence for which can be seen in a document written in the hand of 15-year-old Elisabeth Sharp who styled herself as 'secretary' of Kingarrock and which sets out the 'rules' to be followed by honorary members. The document shows the wit and humour of a slightly cheeky schoolgirl in insisting that honorary members must always ensure that they play with new balls, and must lose at least one ball each round, the approximate location of which must be reported to the 'secretary'; similarly, visitors may only play the course when all members of the family are resting or eating. In a sign of the times, the final rule stated that an honorary member may take along his spouse, but only to caddy for him!

The story of the decline (and re-emergence) of golf at Kingarrock has a mix of family tragedy and national history. Frederick died of a heart attack in 1932. Five years later, on an infamously snowy night, Hugh was tragically killed in the famous Castlecary rail disaster. He was 40, unmarried but on his way to see his new fiancée who lived near Glasgow. It is believed that she had phoned him at the house and persuaded him not to drive but to take the train, due to the atrocious road conditions. Such sound advice unfortunately on this occasion proved fatal as the Edinburgh to Glasgow Express service failed to see the stationary train ahead. Hugh was seated in a first-class carriage at the rear of the train in front and so Frederick's only son died without an heir to the Hill of Tarvit estate.

Perhaps unsurprisingly for the time, the two ladies left living at

Hill of Tarvit (Hugh's mother Beatrice and his sister Elisabeth), allowed the course to revert to farmland, especially as the years of the Second World War required fertile land to be farmed. And so it remained for nearly 70 years until a map was unearthed showing the original layout of the course and by 2008 the 9-hole course was reinstated following roughly the same layout as nearly a century earlier. There are exceptions: in the interests of safety the fairways no-longer criss-cross and players no longer tee off from the lawn immediately in front of the terrace of the house!

Kingarrock remains an incredibly special place and one cannot help but appreciate that where once the privileged family and friends of Frederick and Hugh Sharp played their game, today locals and tourists alike are welcome to visit and use clubs which would have been entirely familiar to the golfers of yesteryear.

A Set of Swilken of St Andrews 'QE2' Limited Edition Clubs

LINDSAY EWART

When the QE2, the world's greatest ocean liner, was to undergo a major refit in 1986, Sandhill (Bullion) Ltd purchased the ship's pair of propellers. Swilken of St Andrews were approached by Sandhill to see if they would be interested in converting their recent acquisition into limited edition sets of golf clubs. This joint venture resulted in 7,500 sets of golf clubs with each club featuring the official QE2 logo and individually numbered. One third went to Japan where they retailed at £6,200.

Lindsay Ewart with Swilken Clubs

Lindsay Ewart at Arbroath had five sets in his Pro-shop: all sold within two weeks, with most people buying them as an investment. Sadly, at a recent auction at Bonham's Chester a set of 3-woods, 9-irons and a putter fetched a mere £225.

Arbroath Artisans

LYNN VALENTINE

Thi club wisnae is swanky is thi ane up thi hill,
bit ma uncle ran thi bar an gowfers o aa sizes
an prices wid cram thirsels in tae thi Artisans.

Thayd playit thir eichteen roons an wir stervin
fir heat, fir beer an cheer, duntin elbas in thir Pringle
jumpirs lik a flock o peacocks hid taen ower thi scene.

A thoucht ma uncle owned it aa—thi green, thi club,
thi dug, thi gowfers themsels. A stood oan halie groond
ahent thi coonter, jist big enouch tae peep alaft thi bar.

A waatchit thim aa, ma lugs tunit in tae thi gowfers
lauchter an boastin. while stuffin ma moo
wi crisps, wi thi wee poke o saut it thi boattom.

A didnae unnerstan thi leid o gowf; nae notion
aboot bogeys ir eagles, bit aa thi same a sneakit oot
tae thi practice green, ma face near tore aff wi thi wund
    fae thi sea.

A sent divots richt intae thi dip; wid nivir mak thi grade,
wid nivir be asked alang thi coast tae Fife ir Carnoustie,
besides back then thi Royal an Ancient didnae let
    lassies play.

Recollections from an Arbroath Artisan Member

BERNIE MORTIMER

Bernie is a 'Son of the Links' being born to a Carnoustie caddie. He caddied at Carnoustie where he was well respected for his skills. During the 2018 Open he featured on an NBC video which triggered a memory in an American golfer for whom he caddied, leading to the two being brought back in to contact. Bernie's golf memories include these two pieces from the *Arbroath Herald*.

Bernie Mortimer

A Fishy Story on Elliott Links
Willie Young and Bernie Mortimer, on volunteer flooding duty last Saturday morning, came across a fish in one of the pools on the fairway.

Discussion took 'plaice' back in the 'smokie' 19th hole as to what species it was. Someone said it must have been a 'mackerel'. After 'floundering' with a few 'red herrings', Doug Hutchinson, the Steward, came to the 'sole' conclusion that it must have been a 'parr'.

Arbroath Herald, 14 March 1977

Notable 'First' for Bernie

Playing in the Sunday Sweep competition, veteran golfer, Bernie Mortimer, recorded his first ever hole in one at the par 3 16th, using a six iron.

His playing partners were these well known Artisan worthies Bob Findlay, Jock Simpson and Frank McDonald. It was reported in the clubhouse afterwards that Bernie, who is renowned for his smooth silky putting stroke, was just relieved that he did not have a short putt for his two. For the record Bernie scored a scratch 69, finishing one, six, three.

Note: *It is also worth noting that Bernie was reported to have smiled after the event!*

Arbroath Herald, 20 August 1993

Bernie Mortimer in action at Panmure Golf Club

That's Golf!

SUSAN GRANT

It sits there, winking mockingly,
that small white orb upon the tee.
I swing my driver mightily.
The ball's still sitting there.

Again I try. I'll not be beat.
This time it goes about five feet
but in a divot takes its seat.
It really isn't fair.

The next hit really isn't planned
to reach that bunker full of sand.
Alas, that's where it's going to land;
a happening not so rare.

Now, if you can, picture the scene.
It's four more shots to reach the green
and when I think what might have been
I groan with deep despair.

So it goes on the whole way round.
My golfing spirit sagged and drowned
and no solution could be found
as I tore out my hair.

Until the last, the eighteenth hole -
par three. My ball did roll and roll
and IN IT WENT! Ultimate goal.
I haven't got a care.

Practice makes perfect!

A Story of Machrihanish Golf Course
Susan Grant

The runway of RAF Machrihanish lies close to Machrihanish Golf Course. When the airfield was in operation and used by the US Navy, a golfer teed off at the 9th hole, skied their drive and hit the fuselage of a landing US plane. It was said that the ball used was a 'Top Flite'!

Royal Dornoch

GORDON BANNERMAN

It regularly features on lists of the world's top links and golfers making the pilgrimage to Royal Dornoch are drawn to the trophy cabinets before and after their round on the Championship Course.

Inevitably perhaps, the extraordinary Carnegie Shield catches the eye, with Dunfermline-born US tycoon Andrew Carnegie – once hailed the wealthiest man on the planet – gifting the trophy in 1901 to a club he joined while ensconced at nearby Skibo Castle.

The Shield is still competed for every summer and is one of golf's most fetching trophies. It features various local scenes crafted in silver and adorned by the Scottish lion and the American eagle. Priceless nowadays, Carnegie paid £120 for the commission.

More eagle-eyed visitors may be drawn to a framed print featuring eight local lads. They grew up caddying on the links for well-to-do, Victorian holidaymakers before leaving these shores to spread the golfing gospel to the United States and Canada.

The legacy of legendary course architect Donald Ross, born in nearby St Gilbert Street in 1874, is apparent in more than 500 courses across the USA, with Pinehurst No. 2 arguably the embodiment of his art.

Ross, who left Scotland in pursuit of fame and fortune in 1899, was far from alone in making his mark on golf in North America. Fellow professional Alex quickly followed in his brother's footsteps, capturing the 1907 US Open in Philadelphia.

Bob Grant, Alex Murray and Don Sutherland are remembered fondly at the club, while the MacDonald brothers – Bob, Bill and Jack – all enjoyed successful pro careers across the pond.

He may have been overshadowed by Donald Ross's alchemy, transforming those virgin landscapes into golden golfing tapestries, but Bob's 1922 victory in the inaugural Texas Open was remembered during the centennial tournament celebrations in San Antonio.

The gold medal from the first tournament may not have remained in the ownership of the family but faded newspaper clippings recall 66 of the top pros gathering in the Menger Hotel ballroom, within a gap wedge of The Alamo, for the awards dinner.

MacDonald left town with $1633 cash in his wallet, having corrected the Junior Chamber of Commerce president, who had suggested he was of Irish descent.

His Florida-based son Bill – born when his three-times married father was 60 – treasures the hickory shaft putter which helped secure the richest cash prize in golf, along with two hickory clubs which had been part of MacDonald's luggage from the Highlands of Scotland to various pro jobs in France and in the States.

While he penned a best-selling coaching book, titled simply *Golf* and a subsequent $1 pocket manual flew off the shelves in the Roaring Twenties, Bob's own life story is quite a tale in itself.

Born in 1885, as a teenager he became accustomed to tramping the links by the Dornoch Firth, caddying for visitors and scrounging clubs to fine hone his competitive skills with contemporaries.

With the wanderlust coursing through his veins, he lied about his age to enlist with the 7th Squadron Scottish Horse for service in the Boer War, only to be captured within weeks of his arrival in South Africa and confined in a prisoner-of-war camp in Pretoria.

Even there, young Bob contrived to win a makeshift golf tournament teed-up in the camp dust, beating Irish Fusilier Pat Toal in the final.

Twenty-one years later, competing at an event in Cleveland, he was reunited over a drink with the beaten finalist, who happened to be among the spectators.

The cherished MacDonald putter also contributed to victories at the Metropolitan Open in 1921 and 1923, and a third-place finish at the US Open of 1915 at Baltusrol.

His power, delivering 300-plus yards off the tee, warranted the nickname 'Long Bob' and attracted a range of endorsements.

Newspaper adverts in 1924 for the 75 cent Pinehurst golf ball promised an extra 25 yards on your drive while the MacDonald name was used in the *Chicago Tribute* to advertise a sale of steel shaft wood clubs for $4.85, if you were quick.

He was a pro at various exclusive clubs and played in the second Masters tournament with Bobby Jones. In 1923, he opened the first 18-hole indoor chip and putt course, on the sixth floor of Chicago's Leiter Building.

After MacDonald retired from tournament golf, he became a renowned coach and found himself in demand among the Hollywood glitterati, including Bing Crosby – who was a visitor to Royal Dornoch in 1971 – Bob Hope, Douglas Fairbanks and Mary Pickford.

In one newspaper article, he recalled playing a round with oil magnate John D Rockefeller on his personal 9-hole course, with the businessman accompanied by no less than five caddies.

An interview with the *Chicago Times* in 1952 hinted at MacDonald's self-deprecating sense of humour.

As Bob remembers it, he was visiting Saint Andrews golf club for the first time when he encountered the late Andrew Kirkaldy, then the patriarch of all Scottish professionals.

They were discussing the greats of the game, when Kirkaldy said, 'Why don't you take a walk down the road and look at the tablet?'

MacDonald investigated and studied its weather torn description: 'Tom Maurice (sic) Jr. 67, 68, 69, 70, 72'. Seeking out Kirkaldy again, MacDonald announced, 'no golfer ever lived who could shoot those scores with the old ball'.

Kirkaldy shook his head in disgust and walked away. Turning back, he snorted, 'Bob MacDonald, you're a fool. Those weren't his scores. Those were the years in which he won the British (sic) Open Championship'.

Bob rubbed shoulders with the greats of the game, including Walter Hagen, Sam Snead, Bobby Jones and Scots-born Open winner Jock Hutchison, while his coaching skills were harnessed by Gene Sarazen and three times US Women's Open winner Babe Zaharias.

Always proud of his Dornoch roots and wider family ties, and no stranger to the bagpipes, MacDonald would take his family along to the annual Highland Games in the Chicago area as a reminder of their Scots heritage.

Beyond Royal Dornoch Golf Club, the name Bob MacDonald has become inextricably intertwined with the history of one of America's oldest and longest-running professional tournaments. His name adorns a bronze plaque at the original Lone Star

State host club, San Antonio's Breckenridge Links, and Bob MacDonald, the lad from Dornoch, will forever be linked with fellow winners of the Texas Open, including Byron Nelson, Ben Hogan, Sam Snead, Arnold Palmer, Lee Trevino, Jordan Spieth and, appropriately, Royal Dornoch honorary members Ben Crenshaw (in 1973 and 1986) and Tom Watson.

Missing the Cut

ANDY JACKSON

I can't shake that tap-in when I lie awake at night,
how I contrived to miss the unmissable putt.
Took my eye off the ball and it slid by on the right.

That 3-wood to the dance floor that just wouldn't bite,
that lip-out on the sixteenth like a punch to the gut,
and I can't shake that tap-in when I lie awake at night.

Fairways cut too narrow, and greens turfed with spite,
hooks I couldn't reason with – that old chestnut.
Took my eye off the ball and it slid by on the right.

Downed a beer with my caddy and promised him I'd write,
but I still hear him laughing outside the scorer's hut,
and I can't shake that tap-in when I lie awake at night.

I read the sporting pages while queuing for my flight,
then phoned my wife and told her how my game was in
   a rut.
Took my eye off the ball and it slid by on the right.

The game gives, the game takes; it still might be alright.
I could take my swing apart and maybe change my irons,
   but
I can't shake that tap-in when I lie awake at night.
Took my eye off the ball and it slid by on the right.

Doug Sanders 1970 Open, St Andrews

In the Bunker

for Paul and Hugh

JULIE McNEILL

I'd fallen asleep when Jack did it
waking, dishevelled in my bed
my dad's eyes glistening
'he did it son, he did it'
not this time.

I am on the verge of manhood now
a mighty thirteen
stoked up on full fat coke
staying up on a school night.

Four feet firmly into Augusta in the springtime
my dad and me commanding the front room.
Golf our religion, and this the high cathedral
as green and pure as the Garden of Eden herself.

Today is Sandy Lyle
six under and facing the big Amen
I can hear whispers of Peter Allis
and great white sharks circling
as he falters.

Calcavecchia's in the clubhouse
and Lyle, in the bunker.
Dad is out of his chair
he's taking the shot,
caddying for Sandy.

'Dink it, son bit of spin,
come in on par, play-offs,
you've not lost it son'
he's looking at me now.

He's swinging for him
his perfect swing
three whiskies in
as Sandy goes for it, over the lip
and
somehow
out of danger
and poised for glory.

We're waiting for the ball to land
for the camera to catch up
the white dot
stops
it rolls
it stops
it rolls.

We creep with it towards the TV
we are the ball
there in the blue and green
the so, so green.

They say Lyle is unflappable
that he 'carries patience in his bag'.
His walk to the ball takes a lifetime
then, with patience, he guides it home.

His arms shoot straight into the air,
the crowd erupts
a victory dance
his dad is there
and mine
is here
whispering this night into my dreams
long after he has gone.

Time stopped that night
I wish that time had stopped that night.

Pete's Greatest Legacy

BOBBY WEED

Named a top island in the continental US (2018 Travel & Leisure), Long Cove Club on Hilton Head Island offers a spectacular Lowcountry setting. This majestic golf course weaves through century-old oak trees covered in Spanish moss, stately Carolina pines and pristine saltwater marshes.

Opened in 1981, Long Cove was my first full-time assignment with Pete Dye. This experience sparked the beginning of a 40-year personal friendship with Pete, as well as my career in design and construction. It was also the genesis of Bobby Weed Golf Design.

Fashioned out of the South Carolina marshes, Long Cove was designed to be a forward-thinking, private residential community with a world-class golf course. After successfully designing nearby Harbour Town Golf Links, Pete was hired as Long Cove's golf course architect. I was appointed as construction supervisor.

Summers in the south-eastern US are brutal. The no-see-ums are unrelenting. Almost no infrastructure is in place at new developments. Long construction hours are the norm. Building golf courses in these conditions is not for the faint of heart. While these impediments may have dissuaded others, Pete always relished the opportunity to design 'in the field'.

Long Cove represents a 'time machine' into Pete's work during one of the most dynamic periods of his career. With its original features, state-of-the-art land plan and colourful history, Long Cove is one of the most significant courses in Pete's portfolio.

The original golf course construction crew at Long Cove is touted as the most successful of the modern era. Consisting of college graduates, interns and low-handicap players alike; many Long Cove alumni would later embark on their own design careers. The team included Pete, me, P B Dye, Tom Doak, Ron Farris and Scott Pool, among others. In the way Pete fashioned his crew, he would typically handcraft his courses and would rarely contract out work. Pete was a great relationship builder. He also had a groupie-like following. People really wanted to work for him.

(L-R) Pete Dye and Bobby Weed

While his physical golf courses will always come to mind, Pete's greatest legacy lives on in the people that he touched, influenced and impacted. Golf course superintendents, architects, shapers, equipment manufacturers and other golf industry professionals were (and remain) the direct beneficiaries of his unwavering work ethic and wisdom.

The two renowned golf course architects and good friends hard at work

When I think of Pete's courses, they were well ahead of their time, and stand the test of time today. He was always on the cutting edge of catering to players in the next generation. While his courses are some of the most difficult for PGA Tour players, he also brought a balance for high handicapper players, aided in part by his wife, Alice.

Pete and Alice were a talented team. She was a fabulous sounding board for him. More often than not, she'd ground Pete when his ideas took on a life of their own. As an accomplished player in her own right, Alice knew first-hand the challenges that female and high-handicap players faced. She represented them well, often working with Pete to achieve his original design goals while simultaneously influencing more forward tees, eliminating forced carries and such…

As a testimony, look at how many of his courses play host to esteemed amateur events, PGA Tour tournaments and Major championships. His architectural balance, variety and interest remain more relevant today than ever. Counted among his courses to host Major events are Crooked Stick – his home course in Carmel, Indiana, multiple PGA Championships at Oak Tree National Golf Club in Oklahoma, multiple PGA Championships, a Ryder Cup, and Senior US Open on The Straits Couse at Whistling Straits in Wisconsin, multiple PGA Championships and two Ryder Cups at The Ocean Course at Kiawah Island near Charleston, South Carolina and a US Amateur and what many call the 5th Major at TPC Sawgrass, the permanent home of THE PLAYERS Championship in Ponte Vedra Beach, Florida, since 1982.

How many memories of great shots have come from Pete Dye courses?

Golf Island

W N HERBERT

Growein up on Gowf Island in mid-Firthstream
we never suspected that there could ever be
sic a game, even though we were gien
oor first flint clubs to swat adders in our cribs,

and, to ease oor teething pains, sooked upon
pitted mint moons. Our handicaps were zero
from infancy wha were raised on mythotopian tales
like oor island's origin wiz in a divot howked

by the giant Hurtigurtiplaiden Pants -
a slice from his redwood club wi an asteroid
for a baa had wiped out aa the dragons
in Angus. They say Young Powrie M'Whakkity

yince sank a hole-in-one in oor ninth
struck from the first tee in the Auld Grey Coorse,
then rowed owre in a skiff and sank
anither in the echteenth at Monifieth.

They say that antic Mr Soth, wha hes played here
since the witch Espair escaped him in a riddle,
yince hit a Pterodactyl on the fourth -
that shot which, though it lands in one in one

hole, can be heard a-rattlin in the next. They say
it dirls and donners still though that micht have been
us teens drinking fool's mead in the bunkers
till we spoke in the tongues of clegs and craneflies.

As soon as we suspected that what we were playing was golf and not, as we'd supposed, zen archery from galloping horseback, we rightly became terrible at it, and soon we took tae Powrie's Skiff.

Amen

GRAHAM FULTON

'Somethin' Stupid'
by Frank and Nancy Sinatra
    is playing as
I stand at the check out
    on Sunday afternoon
with the rain outside
    which makes me think
for a reason known
    to no one
of mum's man JB,
also known as 'Jacky Boy',
  also known as 'Jack',
who would come round
    on Sunday evening
each year
  to watch
the last round
of The Masters
    with a dram in his hand,
a wee goldie with
    a soupçon of water
as we looked at
    the mad dazzling
Georgia flowers,
    the pretty stone bridge,

the heavenly sparkle,
   pristine flat greens
and the towering trees
     completely different
to the lumpy pastures
    of Royal Barshaw
in Paisley, with
long historic shadows
and the crowd yelling things like

       Get in the hole ball!
       or *Get in the ball hole!*
at Amen Corner,
         and we'd have a few more
to keep ourselves company,
mum was happy, until
             the last flag
became a blur
        but it didn't matter
because it was all wonderful
     and I'd sometimes wait
to watch the green jacket
    but I always had work
in the morning, work
   in the morning, and that
was a while ago,
and mum died,
   slowly,
       of cancer
    in the side room
of a silent ward
    in a Glasgow hospital,

and JB fell down and died fast
                as he hit his head
on the doorstep
                of his bowling club, but
I don't think it
                was on a Sunday, it
was something else

Amen Corner

The Youngest Champion – Memories of Nancy Jupp

PETER LOWE

It was Friday, 14 September 1934, and spectators were gathered round the 17th green at Stoke Poges golf club, Buckinghamshire. At just over 4' 6" tall, a 13-year-old girl confidently struck a 5-foot putt into the hole. Nancy Jupp (Longniddry Golf Club) had defeated Joan Montford (North Foreland Golf Club) three and one to win the Girls' Amateur Championship. To this day, Nancy is the youngest winner.

Nancy Jupp was born in London on 29 December 1920 to George and Ethel Jupp and was a younger sister to Rhoda. By May 1921, the family had relocated to Longniddry in East Lothian. George was a senior civil servant in the Ministry of Works. He was born in Clevedon Somerset in 1875 and died in Longniddry in 1938. He played county cricket for Somerset and for Calton Cricket Club in Edinburgh. Although born in England, he Captained the Scotland cricket team. He was a keen golfer and held a handicap of four. Ethel was an actor and opera singer born in Dundee in 1881. She died in London in 1960. She was the first Captain of Longniddry Ladies' Golf Club, where Nancy was a member.

Nancy started playing golf at the age of four. However, a pivotal moment that really caught her interest was attending the 1929 Open Championship at Muirfield and witnessing Walter Hagen sink the winning putt.

Nancy attended school at Edinburgh Ladies College in Queen Street, Edinburgh, where she enjoyed gymnastics, swimming, tennis and hockey. Indeed, her father thought she was a better tennis player than a golfer.

At age 13 years and 259 days, Nancy Jupp won the Girls' Amateur Championship (which was first played for in 1919 at Stoke Poges). Her sister, Rhoda, was thought to be the better golfer and was entered for the event. As Nancy was to travel to support her, she entered as well. The two sisters won their first two matches, but Rhoda was defeated in her third. It was Nancy who was causing a sensation. She was both the youngest and smallest player in the field, but her swing was admired, and she hit the ball a long way. She reached greens in two shots even though they were well over 400 yards. As the week progressed, the press took more interest in her; *The Times* and *The Telegraph* providing significant coverage. One extremely interested spectator was Enid Wilson, who won the championship in 1925. She had gone on to win the Ladies' Amateur in the previous three years and had played in the inaugural Curtis Cup against the USA in 1932. Wilson, who presented the trophy to Nancy, believed that she was the best 13-year-old golfer she had ever seen.

The outcome resonated around the world, with Nancy's victory reported as far away as Argentina, Australia, Iraq and New Zealand.

The Jupp family returned home the following day and received a rapturous welcome in Longniddry. At the Club's annual general meeting a week later, Lord Wemyss, Captain of the club, presented Nancy with a gold watch, and the club professional, William Morris, gave her a new set of woods. In addition, she was made a lifetime honorary member of the club.

To this day, Longniddry commemorates Nancy's achievement. The elm tree on the grass triangle at Links Road was planted in celebration. Yet, years later, Nancy would admit that the fuss

Nancy Jupp in action at Stoke Poges

MIND THE LINKS – GOLF MEMORIES

surrounding her win and the emphasis on her being 'little' had diminished her commitment to the game.

Nancy Jupp, Scottish Girl Golf Champion at 13

Nevertheless, one year later, the Jupp sisters returned to Stoke Poges to play in the inaugural girls' match between England and Scotland. Nancy Captained the Scotland team, which won by five matches to two. Nancy would continue to play in club, county and national events, and in 1953 she won the Women's Amateur Championship of Norway.

During the Second World War, Nancy served in the Women's Auxiliary Air Force. She described herself as a grease monkey servicing Spitfires.

Post-war, she studied journalism and wrote for an English golf magazine before working in Australia. She emigrated to the USA in 1956, where she worked for the USGA, writing press releases and editing the USGA journal. She then became associate editor of *Golf* magazine. She also wrote scripts for the televised series, 'Shell's Wonderful World of Golf'. During her time at *Golf*, she met Ed Carter, a long-time tournament director, who suggested she become a tournament director.

Having taken responsibility for several tournaments, Nancy accepted the position of tournament director at Congressional County Club, Maryland, for the 1964 US Open, which was won by Ken Venturi. In 1967, she was working at Baltusrol when Jack Nicklaus won his second US Open. Her third US Open was at Hazeltine National Golf Club, Minnesota, in 1970 when Tony Jacklin won. She then directed 12 of the subsequent 13 US Opens and performed the same role for the PGA Championships in 1982, 1984 and 1985. She had worked at 19 Major Championships.

When the USGA or the PGA entered into an arrangement for the US Open or the PGA Championship to be held at a golf course, the club was responsible for the logistics for running the tournament. This was a demanding task for a club for which it might not have the necessary experience and expertise. Consequently, the role of tournament director evolved. Nancy undertook this role at 15 US Opens and 4 PGA Championships.

In 1974, the USGA invited Winged Foot Golf Club, New York, to host the 74th US Open on their West course. In turn, Winged Foot employed Nancy as the tournament director. Before that US Open, Jay Searcy interviewed Nancy for his 'Women in Sports' column in *The New York Times*. She stated that the secret to her success was hard work and planning. Indeed, as she spoke, the organisation for the 75th US Open at Medinah had already commenced following Nancy's written instructions over a year in advance.

Nancy had arrived at Winged Foot a year earlier, where she had occupied an office in the clubhouse coordinating the activities of 20 committees made up of 1,200 volunteers from Winged Foot and neighbouring clubs. This was the seventh time that Nancy had carried out this task for host clubs and USGA. She would go on to do it for eight more US Opens and four PGA Championships.

The police officers at the club entrances who check the arrivals' identities and the security staff on the course to ensure safety were all part of this monumental task. Tents of all sizes were procured, and rows of yellow portable toilets were placed at 70 locations, all within the club grounds. Nearby accommodation had been organised for 700 golf officials, players and the international press; television towers for 23 colour TV cameras had been erected. These were connected to $5 million ($28 million at today's prices) of broadcasting equipment by over seven miles of cable buried beneath the immaculately prepared golf course. Provision had to be made for spectator parking, the on-course signage and scoreboards, first-aid stations and the bleachers (stands). Production and printing of the Championship programme was a task of its own.

Catering for the international press was vital and quite different from today. The press tent had to be set up and communication facilities provided. Nancy had procured 200 typewriters, a photo van, radio trucks, telex machines, over 300 phones and six kiosks with IBM monitors, which supplied instant updates and statistics as the tournament progressed, all in stark contrast to the multi-media systems used today.

The 74th US Open became known as the 'Massacre at Winged Foot' and was won by Hale Irwin with a score of 287 (+7).

Nancy had come to respect the US Open at this stage in her

career. She found the atmosphere was different. It opened doors and gave a lifetime of prestige to the winner, saw people from all over the world come together, but what set it apart was the drama, the pathos, the narrow fairways and the deep rough. She thought that there were not many golf clubs worthy of hosting The Open.

Within a month of Hale Irwin sinking the winning putt, Nancy moved to Chicago for the 75th US Open at Medinah. After each championship, she found leaving hard. She worked with many people, got to know them, and appreciated their hard work. There was never a time for loneliness. The job meant that she had to be single and a nomad. Nancy had these feelings 19 times between 1964 and 1986.

In the early 1980s, the USGA took the role of tournament director in house. Nancy handed over the reins to Mike Butz, who became Senior Director at the USGA.

In 1982, Pebble Beach, California, invited Nancy to be Tournament Director at the 82nd US Open. At the same time, she was invited by Southern Hills Country Club, Oklahoma, for the 64th PGA Championship. Nancy decided to do the PGA, which profoundly affected the rest of her life. She bought a condominium in Tulsa and settled, no longer a nomad! Southern Hills granted her lifetime membership privileges in recognition of her outstanding services to golf.

In later life, she joined the senior community at Saint Simeon's Episcopal Home in Tulsa.

Nancy Jupp died on 27 April 2013 at the age of 92. On 1 May 2013, the *Tulsa World* published an obituary in which they described Nancy as an excellent organiser and administrator as a director of golf tournaments and added that she was a very independent and strong-willed person, who never married, and left this world with no living relatives, but with very many friends across the US.

I Think of the Woman Who Dives for Golf Balls

YVONNE GRAY

I think of the woman who dives for golf balls
that gleam on the seabed like fallen moons
struck out-of-bounds, sliced over ancient walls.

Seals flee to kelp forests as a giant pearl falls.
Fish dart from a shadow in primeval lagoons –
crabs scuttle from the woman who dives for golf balls.

A birdie, an eagle, an albatross soars. Each scrawls
a scorecard with dreams, echoes airborne paeans -
not one ball out-of-bounds, sliced over ancient walls.

When salt spray blasts the fairway in squalls
and flags fray, flapping on the greens,
I think of the woman who dives for golf balls.

Herring gulls sail on the wind, cut the air with calls.
They eye circles on water, read the runes –
a ball out-of-bounds, sliced over ancient walls.

When horizons are lost in haar and the ocean brawls
and the airwaves brattle with barbed harpoons,
I think of the woman who dives for golf balls –
how she soars out-of-bounds, free of ancient walls.

A Fox in the Hen House!

LOUISE GRAHAM

Feathers were most certainly ruffled when Billy Casper former Masters and US Open Champion visited Carnoustie Ladies' Golf Club (est. 1873).

It was an ordinary competition day, Tuesday, 12 July 2005, Mr Casper playing down the 18th of the Championship course was informed he was only steps away from one of the oldest ladies' golf clubs worldwide.

Surprise visit by Billy Casper to Carnoustie Ladies Golf Club

'I want to meet all the girls!', was Billy Casper's request, and this he did! The then club Captain, Sheena Seaton, introduced him to many of the stalwarts including Jemmie Greig, Betty Mann, Phyllis Ford and Ann Thomson.

Tea and cake on offer, golf stories were exchanged. Jean Reyner had bragging rights scoring a two on the 2nd hole of the Championship course. Autographs signed, photographs taken, Billy left the clubhouse, generous with his time and compliments to the girls. It was indeed for Carnoustie Ladies' a Glorious Twelfth!

A gift of a signed score card from Billy Casper

I Don't Remember Nicklaus

KEITH McINTOSH

I don't remember Nicklaus
I really wish I did
He ruled the world of golf
When I was just a kid

In Cherry Hills, New Jersey
He faced his first real test
Hogan's on the leaderboard
Can he beat the best?

Palmer was the reigning King
But Jackie didn't care
His reign came to a sudden end
De-throned by the Bear

Other rivals tried their luck
One all dressed in black
They won their share of Majors
But none could equal Jack

Saturday at Turnberry
Jack was in a jam
But even after this defeat
He won another Slam

Nineteen-eighty, Baltusrol
Back atop the pack
The crowd begins to chant aloud
The Golden Bear is back

Seve, Norman, Langer, Kite
All there in the mix
None of them could master Jack
In nineteen-eighty-six

Masters golf at fifty-eight
He was a rank outsider
In the end he finished sixth
Two ahead of Tiger

Which one is the greatest?
I wonder looking back
I've lived the age of Tiger
But I don't remember Jack

Willie's Golf Story

William Douglas Ramsay, 79 Years Young – A Golfing Worthy, born and bred in Carnoustie

LORRAINE YOUNG

'Golf has never just been a game to me, it has been a 'way of life'.

I consider myself to have been blessed to have been born and lived all my life in Carnoustie and been part of a family with a strong passion for the game.

My dad was the first person to encourage and introduce me to the great game and I hope over the years I too have been able to encourage other youngsters to do likewise as golf is a game that can shape you and can mould you throughout your life.

My dad, or 'Basher' as he was known, could not get work during the recession of the 1930s, so he and his friends took up golf. In 1936, he won the Montrose Amateur Open Tournament winning vouchers to spend in the course golf shop. At that time, golf balls were scarce and expensive so, winning the vouchers to buy golf balls, was very welcome.

Dad was a well-known and well-respected golfer across Angus and someone who had, what was described as, a natural talent for the game. He played in the Angus county team and, in 1951, won the honour of being club champion in both Carnoustie Golf Club and Carnoustie Caledonia Golf Club.

Dad won the Craw's Nest Tassie in 1938 and 1939 (prior to the Second World War). This is a highly prestigious Carnoustie amateur competition, attracting an international field. Due to the restrictions that the war brought, he became custodian of the trophy during these years and following my birth in January 1943, I am proud to say the trophy was used as a font at my christening. The service itself took place in my grandparents' home, in James Street, Carnoustie. There is a photo of me sitting in the Craw's Nest trophy but the exact date it was taken is unclear as Dad spent a lot of time overseas during the war years on various postings, including the Far East.

Malcolm Mitchell, was my boyhood friend and he and I were out on the course from sunup to sunset, playing the courses virtually every day during the school holidays. This opportunity to play and experiment our skills provided so much enjoyment and led to a rapid improvement in our overall game.

In July 1953, when I was only 10, I attended The Open at Carnoustie when Ben Hogan made his only Open Championship appearance. Mr Hogan won, making it his third Major championship of the year. When the opportunity presented itself, I politely said, 'Mr Hogan may I have your autograph?' and he obliged! Many others that day were not so lucky, but that one act certainly fuelled my love and desire to keep improving my golf.

One of my treasured memories was becoming a caddie at Panmure Golf Club for a fellow by the name of Howard Thomson. Howard was one of the original family members of the D C Thomson publishing family. I reckon that I would have been approximately 13 when I started caddying for Howard.

Howard was the owner of a unique caddy car and a trailer combination, and I was given the sole responsibility for manoeuvring the whole entourage around the course. This effectively meant that the player walked a lot less than the caddy

Willie Ramsay, past Captain of Carnoustie Golf Club

while I was required to walk round every green and every tee! And on the rainy days, yes, I got a wet behind!

I was paid the princely sum of 7/6d and sometimes, after a good scoring round, up to 8/6d but, more often, I was given a 10-bob note.

Howard was a man of considerable wealth and always treated our family with total respect and always proved to be a perfect gentleman. At this time, only the gentry had a house telephone so Howard would physically come round to our house, knock on the door and ask permission for me to attend as his caddie.

He would always knock on the door at Lingard Street, wait for mum to answer and then, in a gentlemanly way, always lifted his hat and would explain the change in tee-time for the golf game and sought her permission for the new arrangement.

I normally caddied for Howard every Saturday and Sunday but, in the summer season, it was more frequent. One member of his team was a fellow called Captain Spalding, a retired sea captain. As caddies we were always required to stay outside the clubhouse until called forward when we would walk round from the back of the clubhouse to the 1st tee.

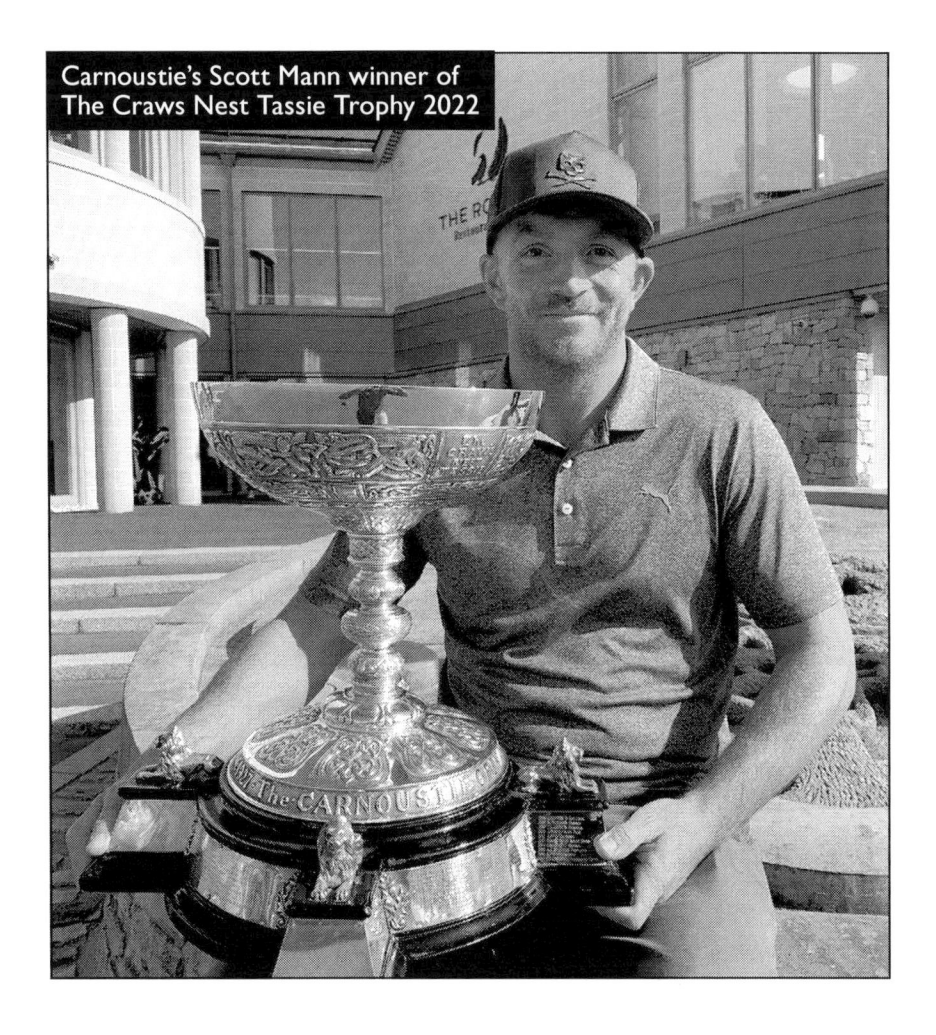

Carnoustie's Scott Mann winner of The Craws Nest Tassie Trophy 2022

If I remember correctly, it was a fellow by the name of Lin Campbell who was the resident professional at Panmure Golf Club in the mid-fifties and if anyone, it is he that I must thank for the initial pairing up with Howard.

Carnoustie Golf Club had a policy of encouraging and supporting youngsters to play the game of golf and as a result I was a loyal member there for all my golfing life enjoying a variety of roles on the committee and as Club Captain 2003-5 and Junior Convenor for several years. I still believe encouraging youngsters to play golf is a great social asset and provides an international passport.

In 1964, I became the Carnoustie Caledonia Golf Club Champion at the age of 21. Over the years my lowest recorded handicap has been 2.

I was privileged during my years at the Carnoustie Golf Club to be their designated correspondent answering queries from overseas of former Carnoustie residents who wished to trace their family history with the club; and many American visitors who had a keen interest in the history of golf associated with Carnoustie. It was a joy and a privilege to do this research on behalf of our honoured guests and visitors to my hometown.

I used to enjoy and look forward to the Carnoustie Winter League which was re-started by the journalist Ralph Duncan after the end of the Second World War. This League is always played out in the harshest of conditions between the end of November and March but is always competitive and enjoys great camaraderie and banter. Ralph worked out the rota/formula for the 20 matches to ensure you played with a different partner each time and then against the others twice.

I was fortunate never to have won the Wooden Spoon, but I am proud to say that I was the overall winner a few times. The

Winter League is still going strong 85 years on and is probably the oldest in the world.

Years later, through my involvement with the county team, I was invited to become chief marshal during the Alfred Dunhill Links Championship – I filled this role for many years. I saw this as a vote of confidence from my peers and deeply cherish this acknowledgement. In 1968, I was honoured to be invited to undertake the role of chief marshal at The Open in Carnoustie.

Again, I was honoured to be asked to be president of the Angus County Golf Association, 2001-2, and played 40 times for them in competitions over the years as well as fulfilling the role of secretary.

These county matches were played at various locations throughout Scotland. Challenge matches with Glasgow were always keenly contested in the early 1960s. There were 12 players in the county team, and they needed 3 or 4 car drivers and cars to get them there. White shirt and club tie were essential accoutrements, plus blazer.

Family conversations in the Ramsay households always tended to centre around golf as my younger brother, David, also known as 'Basher', after dad, was a multiple club champion, quite literally sweeping the boards in 1975.

My nephew, Eric, Basher's son, certainly inherited the family love and natural talent and aptitude for golf. He won on the Challenge Tour, the Australian Amateur Championship in 2005 and in the same year had a memorable Open Championship at St Andrews finishing 23rd, just missing out on the silver medal and has since been made an honorary life member of Carnoustie Golf Club.

Overall, I would say I have had a good life thanks to my involvement with golf. I have met and enjoyed and shared the company of people from all over the world, playing with many golfers, all differing standards but sharing a common bond. For me, there is nothing to beat the feeling of holding a golf club and then hitting the sweetest shot – 'right down the middle'. I might quickly add that this sensation did not happen all that often throughout my career! However, for me what is overarching is, how precious the people, the memories and the ability to recount what golf has done for me, is without doubt, how my life has been shaped.

The Craw's Nest Tassie Trophy

Gary Player at Carnoustie

(July 1968)

JOHN QUINN

The dog days of imperial money
charging two and six to start the journey
for juveniles in off-course tumults
nippers running footloose beyond adults
meeting Bantam Ben's ghost from fifty-three,
mid-Atlantic accents spraying each tee
Arnie's Army, Jacklin, Barnes and Casper
and others puffing at a gasper,
crowds flowing like a babbling burn
the Golden Bear closing on the urn
the Black Knight hitting eagles in the gale
tracking each early leader without fail
and biding his time in the seaside air,
then out of the sunset, by two shots there.

Some Thoughts on Some Stories from Yesteryear

LEE VANNET

My first memory relating to golf that had a real impact on my life was the day I walked into Simpsons Golf Shop (Carnoustie) to ask Trevor Williamson if I could work and help in his shop. It must have been 1979 – I was 12 – and he said, 'yes'.

Simpson's Golf Shop at Carnoustie

I started my journey in golf a number of years before that having been brought up in Carnoustie playing the six-holer – what a fantastic little golf course. As a seven-year-old, I remember getting my first set of cut down hickory clubs for my birthday in a little pencil bag. What a great feeling it was when you then got your season ticket. It was like, 'Wow I've got my season ticket'.

The six-holer, the forerunner to the Carnoustie Buddon Course, is where I fell in love with golf, but most importantly where I learned how to 'golf your ball'. What a great little learning course, I have so many great memories. It's a pity every golf course didn't have something like that; a learning links to grow up on.

I completed my apprenticeship in Simpsons where the primary mission was greeting and selling to the locals and to the many visitors who came to the golf shop.

I made my first golf club when I was 12. It was an Irv Schloss sand wedge and I put it together with a graphite shaft and sold it to, would you believe, my uncle, Jack Grant, and he still has the club. Irv Schloss was the David Leadbetter of his day. In the 1950s, he was probably the leading, or one of the leading, teaching professionals and he produced some clubs which were sold in the late 70s and early 80s.

Another memory is that of looking in the safe of Simpsons, and in the safe, would you believe, there were two amazing pieces of memorabilia. One was the Open medal won by Jack Simpson who was Trevor's great-uncle, Robert Simpson's brother. And the other, was a Titleist 4 golf ball from 1953. Not only was it from 1953, but it was from the very man who won the Open in 1953, the one and only Ben Hogan. And the reason we all know it was his property, was by a little-known fact. In those days, instead of using a Sharpie pen, which obviously you didn't have back then, to identify your golf ball, what Hogan did was he put his thumb nail through the number four on either side of the golf ball. It just goes to show how soft golf balls were. Around that time, the skills and amazing ability of Hogan, to achieve what he did and the stories of his ball striking were quite unbelievable. What incredible memories and what huge motivation for a young kid growing up in that environment.

The atmosphere of the golf shop was amazing. You go through the golf shop and there were thousands of heads; old wooden heads from the 1920s lying in the back of the shop. Simpsons was one of the foremost suppliers of clubs to the world – to America and everywhere else. The legacy of Carnoustie in golf is unbelievable. The number of players who have gone from Carnoustie to America and further afield! Well, the history is out there for everyone to know.

In 1982, I was 14 and playing off a National Golf Club Handicap of two. I used to have a National Handicap and a Club Handicap. Your National Handicap was based on all your scores played in tournament golf away from home. In my opinion, that's a better handicap system than we have now.

The year of 1982 was a pivotal year for me in terms of competing on a national scale, having had some good success county wise. 1982 was my breakthrough year. I remember playing in an Angus county match at Carnoustie and shooting a 68 on the Medal of the Championship course at the age of 14, which was 4 under par and that score helped our team. I think we won the Team Championships that year.

I got my handicap down to two and I entered the Scottish Amateur Stroke Play Championship, which was played that year over Camperdown, and Downfield for the last two rounds. Camperdown and Downfield are two of the finest inland golf courses in Scotland, if not Britain. Camperdown sadly has fallen into a bit of disrepair and neglect. It's no longer a golf course but hopefully someone's going to turn that around because it's got the potential to be world class.

So anyway, the day before the tournament started, I was on the reserve list as first reserve. Philip Walton, who later holed the winning Ryder Cup putt in 1995 at Oakhill, had won the year before. He had won the Scottish Amateur Stoke Play in 1981 and he had pulled out the day before the tournament started, which meant I, being first reserve, could get into the tournament – fantastic.

LEE VANNET
Scottish Boys Champion 1983
British Boys Champion 1984
Scottish Internationalist

SCOTTISH BOYS STROKE PLAY 1st BARASSIE 1983

SCOTTISH BOYS STROKE PLAY 3rd CARNOUSTIE 1984

SCOTTISH BOYS MATCH PLAY RUNNER-UP DUNBAR 1984

Lee Vannet's awards and medals

EUROPEAN BOYS TEAM ROYAL ST GEORGES 1984 WINNERS

LEVEN GS AMATEUR CHAMPIONSHIP RUNNER-UP 1984

SCOTTISH OPEN AMATEUR STROKE PLAY RUNNER-UP BLAIRGOWRIE & LANDSDOWNE 1984

BRITISH BOYS CHAMPION ROYAL PORTHCAWL 1984

I got picked up on the Saturday morning by the one and only David Greig – legendary golfer from Carnoustie, Scottish Boys champion, Scottish Amateur champion and short game guru.

Lee Vannet with trophy

Can you imagine getting picked up by a Scottish Amateur champion, one of the players for whom you have the utmost respect? I played a lot of golf with David on Saturday mornings. Sometimes when I got a game, my father played with Davy Greig, Willie Ramsay and David 'Basher' Ramsay – both local heroes but David Greig was a national champion, so he was in a higher level in terms of achievements. He picked me up and drove me to Camperdown where we both played that day.

I shot a 72, I recall, and at Downfield in the afternoon, I think I shot 71 to make the cut, which was obviously the first goal, but a great achievement to shoot under par in our national event. Thus I got to play the last two rounds with the one and only Ryder Cup Captain, European Tour Order of Merit winner for seven years, Colin Montgomerie – 'Monty'.

David Greig

Monty's got this huge Tournament pro-bag, which his brother is carrying for him, and he's just been beaten in the final of the English Championship. I'm standing with him with a little tiny leather pencil bag with a set of clubs that, if you didn't know any better, looked like they were rusty and falling to bits…except, they were some of the best clubs ever made – a set of McGregor Tourney Tommy Armour irons. The chrome was coming off, but they were just fantastic. I used an old John Letters Golden Goose putter, which, if you looked at the size of it, was barely bigger than the ball. Now the ball was the small one-point-six-two-inch ball, so I must have looked a real sight. I shot 80 in the third round and 73 in the final round and finished 10th or 12th as a 14-year-old. If I had shot 73 in the third round, I believe I would have won it. That was a great achievement and a wonderful experience playing with Monty who obviously went on to bigger and greater things.

On the basis of my performances that year, especially in that event, I was picked for the Junior World Cup which was played at the Atlanta Athletic Club – one of the many homes of the famous Bobby Jones. Bobby Jones grew up at East Lake Golf Club. Stewart Maiden, affectionately known as 'Kilty Maiden' (I guess he must have worn a kilt), a native of Carnoustie, was the golf professional at East Lake. Bobby Jones honed his golf and his swing by imitating and watching Maiden. The famous Carnoustie swing was huge in America. MacDonald Smith, another Carnoustie man, was also famed for his golf swing. There is a Bobby Jones room at East Lake Golf Club and all his memorabilia and trophies are there.

For me to get to play in the Junior World Cup in a two-man team representing Scotland, was a great honour. And I did so in September, in the humidity of Atlanta, playing at the site of the 1976 US Open won by Jerry Pate who famously held his second shot at two feet at the last, holing it for a birdie to win. Every night that week, or on at least three nights, all the countries were given a talk. The first night was Larry Nelson, US PGA Champion, who talked about his life, how he had been in Vietnam and taken up the game at 21. He had learned his golf from a book by Ben Hogan. There you go, funnily enough, another Carnoustie connection. The next night was Tommy Arron who had won the Masters in 1973. He talked about his upbringing and his life and how he got good. What tremendous motivation for anyone at that age or at any age to be given access to ask questions of some of the greatest players ever. It was fantastic. The prizegiving was something to behold. You can imagine a ballroom inside the Atlanta Athletic Club. They had 20 tennis courts at the golf club, the country club had two huge Olympic sized swimming pools, the locker room in the golf club was bigger than most people's golf clubs. They had a bar attendant in the locker room! This was 1982. You can only imagine what it's like now. On the last evening, Byron Nelson stood up and gave a speech and presented all the prizes. I got to meet Nelson and shake his hand. What an amazing man and what an amazing experience for someone just turned 15 – to get away across to a new land and mingle with the best players in the world.

José María Olazábal played for Spain that year. I would go on the following year to play against him in a Great Britain, Ireland and European team match at Glenbervie Golf Club where The Boys Amateur Championship was held. I remember rolling a putt down from 30 feet to a foot to tap in to win on the last green against Olazábal in a foursomes match.

MacDonald Smith, who was mentioned earlier, was one of the famous Smith brothers. He was the most famous although he never won a Major whereas both Alex and Willie won the US Open. Almost all of MacDonald Smith's winning medals were bequeathed to Carnoustie Golf Club, and they are there to this day. It's an amazing collection of medals. MacDonald Smith was regarded as one of the finest ball strikers of his day with one of the finest techniques.

Lee Vannet

MIND THE LINKS – GOLF MEMORIES

My Golfing Pal

OLIVE M RITCH

Poor Pete didn't play well.
He started with a triple bogey
and blamed his glasses,
the morning sun.

Then his ball went out of bounds
and he cursed the gorse for hiding it
and drawing blood. He played on
and duffed the next shot.

Not his best day, poor Pete,
but I excelled with a birdie,
an albatross and a hole in one
at the eighteenth. Yes, amazing,

and like you say, the same as last week.
Poor Pete did not join me for a snifter
in the clubhouse. Speechless, I
watched him drive off at speed

in his ten-year-old Fiesta
with his head down.
Yes, a bad loser. It's only a game,
after all, just a bit of fun.

Rory McIllroy searching for his ball at 148 Open Championship in 2019

Murdo

LEELA SOMA

green, green, grass against the blue, blue, blue sea
grass and sea, ball and club, perfect strokes
sound of the sea, on West Sands coming over the wispy
   grasses

glorious international game bringing the world to
   The Open
from maharajahs to humble Joe Bloggs, the crisp crack
   of club
against the tiny ball, teeing off the wave like green, bated
   breaths

watching countries mighty and small attempt a five
   hundred year old
game invented by Scots, the wood & iron take pride of
   place.
Alfred Dunhill Cup, 1966, Colin Montgomerie capped
   veteran

memory etched in the mind of the Indian team, ranked
   596 in the world
upsetting all, winning the round, media frenzy in black &
   white
read all over. 'India upsets Scotland in Dunhill Cup match'

makes huge headlines. Golf history made on The Old
   Course, a win
tracing connections between two countries entwined in
   colonial
binds reaching over four hundred years of love & hate,

pride & joy, trade & skills, tea & jute, connections over
   centuries
St Andrews churches in India, Madras College on the
   Fife coast
winners and losers of an ancient game, a kind swap.
   Chess from India
golf from Scotland, sport that transcends countries,
   embraces all.

The Man I Called Nana

CHARLES D BURGESS

After my great-grandmother died suddenly in 1947, my parents and I moved into the simple five-room cottage on the grounds of the Woodland Golf Club in Newton, Massachusetts, where my great-grandfather, the club's retired golf professional lived alone. I called him 'Nana'.

I should explain how a world-renowned Scottish-born golf pro and former professional football player was known as Nana. My great-grandfather, Charlie – 'Chay' to his associates in the golf world – was affectionately known as Nana in our family thanks to my father who as a very young child mistakenly called his grandfather, and not his grandmother, Nana. I grew up thinking that the term Nana, as it applied to my great-grandfather, was a perfectly normal term of affection for him.

Chuck Burgess with his great-grandfather Chay Burgess

I have many wonderful recollections of Nana and my childhood at 'the club'. I remember one cold and crisp October morning in 1952 when the sun was low and shining brightly across the 18th fairway making the frost sparkle like diamonds on every blade of grass. That day, like every other day that year, my great-grandfather took my small hand in his and walked with me along the 18th fairway to my elementary school. I was seven years old. At the end of the school day, he was waiting for me on a bench next to the 17th green for the walk home to our small cottage near the 1st tee. He did that every day, in every weather, for as long as I lived with him. It is a cherished memory that has been with me for 70 years; I loved him more than anything.

Growing up on a golf course provided me with unique and special experiences. Once a week in the summertime, I would walk across a small meadow separating our cottage from the imposing Woodland clubhouse to see Nana's friend Percy, the kindly Jamaican-born chef at the club. The club's service entrance was directly across from the back door of the cottage. Percy would fill up a large bowl with assorted scoops of ice cream from the kitchen freezer for Nana and me. He carefully covered the jam-packed bowl with a large paper napkin to protect it from bugs and the hot sun for my return trip back to the cottage through the wildflowers and tall grass. My great-grandfather's favourite flavour was 'Frozen Pudding' and mine was 'Peppermint Stick'. We sat at our chipped porcelain kitchen table, picking pieces of stuck paper napkin from the slowly melting ice cream scoops as we ate the special treat.

The uninsulated cottage was very hot in the summer and very cold in the winter. The floors were covered with worn linoleum and the simple bathroom featured a small claw foot tub – no shower. In the hot summer months, long before the age of air conditioning, I ran under the giant irrigation sprinklers on the fairways to cool down. One summer day, a heavy rainstorm provided my father with a rare opportunity. He put on his bathing suit, grabbed a bar of soap and used the rain to take a refreshing shower behind the cottage. As that big summer storm went on, it turned to hail, and the combination of rain and frozen hailstones filled a hollow between several grassy bunkers becoming a very chilly swimming pool for me.

I often looked for lost golf balls in the rough and woods along the course, my dad and Nana pointing out the most likely hazards where an errant shot might land. Like most boys in the 1950s, I played cowboys and Indians in the woods, often with my cousin Jerry when he visited. Sometimes I invited a classmate from school to play and we spent hours trying to catch the frogs, turtles and giant goldfish that populated the water hazards on the course.

At night before bedtime, I would say my prayers, climb into bed, and with his delightful Scottish brogue, listen to Nana tell me exciting tales about our family home and the farms of Montrose. My favourite story was about when we would some day travel together by steamship back to Scotland where a beautiful black Shetland pony was waiting for me at our family farm by the sea.

Even as a young boy I knew that Nana was a special person held in high esteem by everyone who knew him. Famous golfers, sports stars and show business celebrities whose names I cannot recall would call upon him at the cottage, on the course or at his old pro shop.

When he died in 1960, I was teenager and had never experienced such a profound loss. It left a hole in my heart for a long, long time. As an adult, I began to learn, and importantly, understand what the man I called Nana meant to others and the remarkable things he did for the game of golf.

Charles M 'Chay' Burgess was born in 1873 in Montrose, Scotland, home to the world's fifth oldest golf course, and was an amateur golfing prodigy who also excelled in football. At 15, he became the youngest player on the then amateur Montrose Football Club and later played professional football for Dundee, Millwall in London, Newcastle United and Portsmouth Football Club.

At 28, he was appointed head professional of the Royal Port Albert Golf Club and later became superintendent of the ancient Montrose Links. He was elected to the Professional Golfers' Association in 1904 and competed against The Great Triumvirate – British Champions Harry Vardon, James Braid and J H Taylor. His exceptional talent, however, was an insightful ability to quickly teach a beginner the essentials of the game.

Chay came to America in 1909, recruited by the Woodland Golf Club in Newton, Massachusetts, where he remained as professional for the next 35 years. There he discovered and mentored 15-year-old caddie Francis Ouimet who became 'America's first golf hero' when he stunned the golfing world by winning the 1913 US Open defeating British legends Harry Vardon and Ted Ray. Ouimet also won the United States National Amateur Championship in 1914, and again in 1931 with Chay Burgess at his side. Chay taught two more American National Amateur Champions – Jesse Guilford in 1921 and Ted Bishop in 1946.

During golf's off-seasons, Chay became the first professional coach of soccer at Harvard University. He coached Harvard from 1909 until 1922 winning back-to-back National Collegiate Championships in 1913 and 1914.

Throughout his career at Woodland, he apprenticed many

future American pros including his son Charles II and his seven nephews, Harry, Bert, Willie, Charlie, Jimmy, Frank and Arthur Nicoll. Bert Nicoll became head pro at Pinehurst and at the Palm Beach Country Club. Charlie joined Bert at the famous Southern US resorts, and Willie wound up at the Peninsula Country Club in California as the teacher of Amateur Champion Lawson Little.

Chay was among the first Scottish born professionals who had belonged to the PGA in Britain before emigrating to America and he had great concern for the working conditions of club-based teaching professionals in the United States. Soon after the PGA of America was established, he founded the independent New England Professional Golfers Organization (NEPGO) in 1921, a regional professional organisation for teaching pros rather than one focused on national touring professionals. Under his leadership, the NEPGO won wide acclaim for the social and professional benefits gained for its more than one hundred regional members, one tenth of the entire PGA of America. It was also the first professional golfers' organisation in the nation to reach out to women amateurs for coed amateur-pro events. The PGA of America quickly revised its constitution to support club pros nationwide and the NEPGO voted to affiliate with the PGA. Chay Burgess, by unanimous vote, became the first president of the New England PGA in 1922.

Another legacy of my great-grandfather was his influence on the fledgling Ryder Cup competition. After the inaugural Ryder Cup matches at Worcester, Massachusetts, in 1927, the PGA of America did not have enough money to send an American team to England for the return match and to defend the Cup. In 1928, he arranged an impressive fundraising tournament in support of the team, featuring the greatest golfers of the day and all former

US Open Champions. Chay was the Grand Marshall of the event and Francis Ouimet refereed the match pitting Walter Hagen and Gene Sarazen against reigning US Open Champion Johnny Farrell and the incomparable amateur Bobby Jones. The efforts of Chay and his fellow professionals raised over $10,000, enough money to ensure that the 1929 trip to England was funded, thus saving the Ryder Cup competition from an early demise.

...

Nana passed away in 1960. In 1999, I finally made that trip to Scotland. My travelling companion and fellow researcher was my wife, Catherine. Together we met Scottish relatives, golf and football historians, and made many new friends. We visited museums, libraries, golf societies and other places throughout the UK where Nana once lived, worked and played. His impact upon the game of golf, both amateur and professional, as well as his influence on early American collegiate soccer became clear. It became the inspiration for my first book *Golf Links – Chay Burgess, Francis Ouimet and The Bringing of Golf to America*, celebrating the important work of golf's unsung club professionals, like Nana, who taught the world the game of golf.

Where Have all the Golf Balls Gone? Long Time Passing

EUAN KERR

Titleist, Callaway, Srixon – all favoured golf balls today but never heard of in my young days as a golfer in the 1950s. I've often wondered whatever happened to the rich array of golf ball brands from these halcyon days back then. They seem to have disappeared off the face of the Earth.

There were, of course, the top brands like the Dunlop 65, Slazenger Plus and that 'happy' golf ball the Penfold – often seen with a 'smile' on its face due to its wafer-thin cover. Then there were the second-grade balls like the Dunlop Warwick and the Bromford (Penfold's second string ball). Dunlop even had a third-grade ball, the unfortunately named Dunlop Bogey (the marketing manager should have been sacked for that one).

It's the lesser-known balls that I remember best, the likes of the Saxon, Demon, Spitfire (which often went down in flames), Mercury, Meteor, Blue Spot, the list goes on. Two balls that no self-respecting golfer could play without the risk of being mocked by his peers were the low-grade Commando and the GBD (it stood for Golf Ball Development).

I'll throw in a quick quiz question here. Which two golfers from the past had golf balls named after their scores? Award yourself a coconut if you said Henry Cotton and Bobby Locke. Dunlop 65 was named after Henry's astonishing 65 score in the 1934 Open at Sandwich and the Slazenger 279 named after Bobby Locke's four round total in the St Andrews Open of 1957.

Back to obsolete golf balls. Does anyone remember the Price's Everlasting ball? You would think with a name like that, it would still be around today, but no.

I also have fond memories of finding a much sought-after Silver King *gowfie*. Sadly, it met a watery grave in the burn on the fourth on Carnoustie Burnside – always a mighty carry for a puny nine-year old.

'Anyone got a scoop?'

The brothers Mann, Wallace, Fraser and Lindsay lived yards from the Carnoustie golf courses, and all became professional golfers. As youngsters they used to love it when there had been a downpour on Friday night leaving the Barry Burn a muddy torrent for the Saturday golfers. At dawn on a Sunday morning, they would get up and trawl the now clear burn for the balls that had taken the plunge during the previous day. Rich pickings indeed.

So where are all these long-forgotten brands? Well, my theory is that all the balls that landed in the likes of the Barry Burn at Carnoustie and the Swilken Burn at St Andrews eventually made it down to the sea.

They found Shackleton's ship the *Endurance* on the bottom of the ocean after over a hundred years. Perhaps one day they'll dredge the bottom of the Mariana Trench – the deepest point of all the oceans and discover a monumental stash of previously loved golf balls. If they do, I'm claiming the Silver King.

Formative Years at Carnoustie

DAVID BLAIR

I was born in April 1933 and have lived in Dundee Street here in Carnoustie all my life. I have lived in three houses, all of them a mere stone's throw from the 18th green of our famous golf course.

David Blair

My father was a keen golfer, and it was he who encouraged me to take up the game. The majority of my peers also played golf and during the summer we were never far from the Links.

A junior season ticket for the Burnside course cost seven shillings and six pence for the year or alternatively, if you couldn't afford a season ticket, a fee of six pence for every round played.

I fondly remember one Burnside starter who would quietly lay aside our six pences, each of which should have paid for a single round, and when she had accumulated enough to pay for a 7/6 season ticket, she would hand one to us. On reflection, this was a woman who wished to promote junior golf in Carnoustie.

The photograph showing me standing behind the trophy display was taken in 1947. The trophies, from left to right, are the Nicol Cup, the Arbroath High School Medal, the Junior Links Championship and, in front, the Francis Gallet Golf Bag.

It was a rare event for an individual to hold the Nicol Cup and the Junior Links in the same year. Juniors aged 13 and under competed for the Nicol Cup and juniors aged 14 and over competed for the Junior Links Championship. However, by virtue of my birthday falling on a certain date and the fact that I was unusually tall for my age, my entries were accepted without question for both competitions and as they say, 'the rest is history!'

The Francis Gallet Golf Bag was a one-off, knock-out competition for junior golfers playing out of the Carnoustie Golf Club. Francis Gallet was a Carnoustie born professional golfer who, like so many talented golfers of his generation, travelled to the US to compete on the professional golfing circuit. During one of his many home visits he presented this prize, and I was lucky enough to prevail on that occasion. I recollect that the bag was relatively compact and not too heavy so a useful addition to my locker.

The trophy haul from 1947 did not end there. That same year, I won the Junior County Championship that was played over the Burnside Course here in Carnoustie. Previously, there had been no trophy awarded to the winner, however, on this occasion, the County Committee felt that the winning round should be fittingly marked, so a trophy was hastily bought from a Carnoustie jeweller and presented to me that same day.

If I were to be asked what the pinnacle of my adult golfing career was, I would have to say winning the Carnoustie Golf Links Championship in 1960 at the age of 27 where I can be seen enjoying a celebratory drink from the trophy after the presentation.

It is fair to say that I peaked early in my golfing career, and though I no longer regularly play the courses which have played such a significant role throughout my lifetime, it is still pleasurable to recall past glories with friends down at the clubhouse on a Saturday afternoon over a glass or two of the amber nectar.

Elegy for Peter Alliss

ANDY JACKSON

In my inner game
I hear that voice –
the amiable duffer,
unreconstructed,
every observation
underclubbed in an
overclubbed world.

A short chip away from the
18th Green at Carnoustie

Bow Before the King of the Windmills

STEPHEN WATT

It was never my sport
but give me *Crazy Golf*
and I'd tear you a new throat.

Ripping open our Velcro wallets, we deposited
fifty pence for a stick and a ball.

Our pink paper ticket entitled us not
to a metal head, a club, nor a putter,
it
was a stick   to whack   into a hole.

We galloped, bolting round obstacles,
tunnels, tubes and ramps,
scudding turf and swamps and tracks,
then divots of grass
and shards of glass,
laughing our arses off when the fat attendant
gave chase.
            It was an easy race to win.

Shin-deep in duck ponds,
I grew fond of the game.
I began studying every bend,
moat house, loop-de-loop,
ever present
in the snow, wind and rain.

And then I swear, by the name of God,
I chipped the ball over the metal chain
which the windmill prop caught
and like some slingshot,
tossed it
straight into the hole.

An old man and his dog were the only onlookers.

Nobody would believe me
and evidence was scarce
so aged ten, I retired,
put on my bravest face,
and turned my hand to snooker.

How to Punch

VICTORIA McNULTY

Mud stuck trainers slunk a wire cut hole,
A burn ribboned wae white puckered balls
Doubling as a sparra's bath.

A think ae you in 501s
Mair cans than clubs.

Your life just Pink Floyd and nae dreams
Free labour on Youth Training Schemes.

A waster. A Thatcher wean.

A diamond in the rough
Of a Glasgow Corporation golf course.

Naebody taught you how to punch,
Loved and sun-kissed sipping wae your pals
In that endless City of Culture summer.

That city was faltered
Wae dole queues and shipyards shuttered
Warrant sales and motorways choking her dry.

A know why,
In that leaf veined yellow light of the Lethamhill side
You chose to swing your way and hide.

Golf in my Veins

A CARNOUSTIAN

In an interview, George Lowe, reminiscing about his early life in Carnoustie in the 1860s, said any child brought up in the town could not help but be infected by the golf virus. In an interview with Bernard Darwin for his book on James Braid, Braid said something similar about Earlsferry. The 'game' is simply infectious!

I was born in Carnoustie High Street in May 1944. My relationship with the game of golf began in Hunters Town, part of the old Balskellie estate, located just beyond the old Corner Hotel, only becoming part of Carnoustie at the end of the Second World War. My early childhood memories are like flashes of black and white, sometimes colour photographs. So, I would ask my mother, father and grandparents about them, mainly when I was approaching my teenage years.

Both my parents worked. I was brought up until around the age of five by my grandparents during the day in their linked cottage, belonging, I believe, to Pitskelly Farm. There were two attached cottages on the left-hand side of the road, directly across from Sheriff Boan's detached villa, a monkey puzzle tree in his garden. My granny and grandad were in the cottage next to Len Dobson's radio and TV shop.

Before the age of three, my grandfather, Tom, gave me a cut-down golf club and a ball. My golf course at my granny's back door was a path that ran between two vegetable patches. It was roughly 25 yards long with a drying green at the bottom on the right-hand side and fruit bushes growing an abundance of blackcurrants and gooseberries on the left-side. The path was my golf course, although I had no idea what a golf course looked like.

I was not that accurate, my ball landing nearly halfway down in the lettuce or carrots and worse, the Brussels sprouts, my small footprints providing the evidence. Tom would come home from his part-time job as a gardener at Smieton's jute factory to find my footprints: 'Try not to hit your ball to the right, let me see you hit another.' I remember his words as if it was yesterday. This encouragement was all that was needed!

I was a chubby wee boy. I barely survived, however, that winter of 1947, one of the coldest on record, as I ended up with double pneumonia and temperatures around 104. Dr McConnel eventually acquired penicillin tablets which probably saved my life. I was told much later, due to the illness, I went from being chubby to skinny and at a time of rationing.

Grandfather Tom was an imposing man just over six feet tall, ex-military, wounded in the service of the Queen – Victoria, that is. Tom would explain things in a way I could understand, and I felt safe with him. He was my surrogate dad. He often took me on long walks where we would stop at a place known as Cowbyres and we would return by the same path. During these walks, I would see golfers playing, and Tom would fill my head with stories about Carnoustie players of old and foreign players who had graced these links.

Before the end of the summer of '49, my grandfather and I played part of the 1st, then all of 2nd, part of the 4th and then the 5th holes on the Burnside course. I could look forward to a bottle of juice, Smiths' crisps and two egg bridge rolls at the 'Hut' beside the eleventh tee of the Medal course. I can't remember the old man's name who looked after us in the 'Hut', but I don't think he took much money as he put more food into a brown paper bag to see us on our way.

While my early life might have been dominated by golf memories with my grandfather, it wasn't the only activity I remember. My granny used to take me to the beach. According to her, we would spend a long time there on sunny days. I remember being dumped in a cold shower and told to wash the sand off. I had been in the water and was taken up into Ferrier's beach changing station beneath the Beach Café for a shower. Not a pleasant experience, the water was cold!

By the time I was six, golf was a regular feature with my grandfather. So off we would go when he came home from work. Tom would make sure no one was on the first tee, a wave to the starter, and off we would go playing from the fairway onto the first green, then the second tee with its shot over the burn, which no longer exists. Tom would always wear his tweed jacket and have his clay pipe firmly stuck out the side of his mouth.

When I was seven, we played with hickories. Still a skinny wee lad, my clubs were a bit too long in the shaft. I had a driver, a yellow-headed spoon, three irons and a brass-headed putter in a homemade canvas carry bag with a small pocket for tees and balls. The bag was mysteriously made in two factories – Smieton's and Anderson & Grice. I had a mixture of golf balls: Spitfire, Warwick, and if I found one, a prized Dunlop or two. None of my golf balls was purchased from Simpson's shop, but I might get a new Dunlop 65 in my stocking at Christmas instead of an orange.

By 1953, at nine years of age, I played the full 18 holes of the Burnside golf course. If I remember correctly, the cost of my round of golf was fourpence in old money, although it might have been tuppence, I didn't pay! Nevertheless, I was obsessed with golf.

July 1953 was also a big year for Carnoustie. The Open would be played over the Medal course. The Burnside course was also used for qualifying. For a nine-year-old, the town was hard to describe, even before Open week. Some 'big names' were already in the town's environs. I took myself across the links via the cinder path to the 9th hole where I saw Bobby Locke playing wearing a pair of brown cords and a sweater, not what I'd seen from the colour photographs I had of him in plus fours and a blue jacket. I heard Hogan was practising at the Panmure Golf Club. However, too much was going on in the town to cycle to Barry Links on a rumour.

My mum was an assistant chef at the Aboukir Hotel run by a Mr Adamson, a French chef, originally from Largs in the west of Scotland. Three days before The Open was due to start, we had visitors. I looked out our front window to see this great big blue and white American car drawing up outside our front gate and my mother getting out. A young girl followed, carrying a baby and a tall gentleman. I took them to be American.

I opened the front door and was introduced to Mr & Mrs Prevatt. They would be staying with us for the week of The Open. They had travelled from Germany. Mr Prevatt was a Captain in the USAF. They had left Germany thinking it would be simple to get a room in a hotel near the town. But, according to my father, they would have been lucky to get one in Edinburgh, 70 miles away! My father was ex RAF – plenty for them to talk about! They had turned up in Carnoustie on someone's suggestion they might get a room at the Aboukir. Captain Prevatt had travelled all those miles to see one man – Hogan!

During the qualifying rounds, I walked down the cinder path, reaching the third tee on the Burnside course. Two or three adults were standing watching as a group came off the second green, two British and one American – I could tell by how he dressed. I was carrying my small autograph book, nothing to show for it at that point. As this tall Yank started walking towards the tee, one of the adults whispered to me, 'Do you know who that is? It's Frank Stranahan'. At this point, the third green was still occupied. Stranahan walked straight up to me. 'Hi, what's your name?' I told him. 'Is that your autograph book?' 'Yes.' He took it from me. 'Where are you from?' 'Carnoustie', I said. 'Do you play golf? Silly question', I thought he said and signed my book. I said, 'Thank you, sir', as he handed it back.

Then, as I was so close to the third tee, I remember he pulled out a 7-iron – the blade was like polished steel, but the shaft was a strange yellow colour – and pushed a tee peg into the ground. It almost vanished. He didn't really have a practice swing and sent the ball towering into the blue sky. I watched as it seemed to cover the flag, landing just beyond in the middle of the green behind the flag. I don't know how far that shot went. The tee was pushed as far back as it could go short of going onto the second green. I was a fan! Frank would go on to tie in second place. It was also a lesson I would never forget

I saw Hogan play out on the Medal course. The crowds following him were huge, making it hard for a wee laddie to get close enough. But I did manage on the sixth tee amongst a group of three or four young lads not much older than me. I thought he hit a brassie, or 3-wood in today's language, a powerful hit down the left, eventually moving into the fairway. It looked like a 1- to a 3-iron for the next, but I guessed as I played with hickory clubs!

I tried to see Hogan come down the last in the final round.

The crowd was enormous. I could see him with his caddie, but I never saw him reach the green. However, I had seen Eric Brown. Again, adults were pointing out players to me. Dai Rees, Fred Daly and De Vicenzo, to name three. I was the babysitter in the evenings while my dad took the Prevatts out for meals ending up in the Carnoustie Club.

I practised almost every day between the ages of 14 and 15. Some days after tea, I would go down around 7pm and play around to the 14th hole and practise till 10pm. One night, a ghostly figure came out of the gloom: 'What are you doing out so late?' It was Gordon Spankie. I noticed that he was smartly dressed in blazer and pressed trousers. He stood and watched me hit some more balls, then said it was time for me to go home and walked with me to where there was street lighting at Golf Street.

After leaving school at the age of 15, my life in golf changed. In Dundee, David Low's sports director interviewed and offered me an apprenticeship in their golf shop at Carnoustie. All the ramifications of what my life would be like were explained to me. I was excited to start, but my father stopped me from taking the position. It was also the year my grandfather died. We still had our round of golf occasionally. However, he fell a couple of times on the golf course breaking his pipe and swearing me to secrecy.

And so, my early life in Carnoustie proved I would be properly infected by for the rest of my life by the golf virus.

1984

GRAHAM FULTON

me and my brother
eating a packed lunch
in the dunes the sand

wondering
if we should
go down to the water
nd run in the surf
like Eric Liddell
or Ian Charleson ghosts
of the dead those

still to die

or should we
follow a big name
or sit in a stand
and watch them all their lives
our stories unfolding
before us so
we sit
at a short par 3
and they're
strolling past
a few yards away
waving smiling
and here's Jack Nicklaus
Lee Trevino Fuzzy Zoeller

Greg Norman Fred Couples
and last of all Tom Watson
with their shoes
and their slacks
and the seagulls
and the people cheering
and clapping and eating
their packed lunches
drinking their drinks
clicking their snaps
wearing their hats

the light in
our eyes suddenly

everyone
is following
the final pairs
and we're trying
to catch a glimpse
of what's going on
but the crowds
are too big the people
are too fast we race
to the end
and wait at the side
a perfect view balanced
on a fence
a garden fence
a Royal and Ancient
metal spike
the flying flags
the valley of sin

Seve Ballesteros – That Winning Feeling

the sound of the hands
on the clubhouse clock trying

not to fall
before our time

and my brother
opens a can of beer
and soaks a man

and the crowds
at the eighteenth
are on their feet
as Seve Ballesteros
is punching the air
again and again
in the Fife sun the Spanish
sun
the wind from the North Sea
the clouds the green
the sound of the sky
the din of joy
with his black hair white shirt
dark blue jumper
and dreamlike immortal
smile
the claret jug
in his hands
forever the moment
is now we catch

the bus
all the way
back to Paisley see
if we can find ourselves on
the late-night news a tiny blur
at the edge
of someone
else's memory

Golf For All

ANDREW MURRAY

'I got a six mummy. The first time I got a seven, then a seven and the last time a six.'

I've just been out on the golf course with my oldest, Nina. She's able to connect with the ball, but actually got a six throwing the ball towards the hole. She's excited having learned about bunkers, tees and greens, and relays this expert knowledge to Jennie, my wife, and Fran aged five and Sonny aged three. Now Fran is desperate to play, and we agree to go tomorrow. Fran is even more pleased to hear granny and papa can join and play with us.

That's the thing about golf. You get fresh air, are guaranteed exercise, and we know these things are good for mental health and physical health. The science is consistent and growing. But it can also provide social connections, and a chance to play with anyone. I can play with my daughters and my parents, who played with their parents, brothers and sisters as well as friends.

There is also the challenge of golf. I enjoy golf without ever breaking 80, but there is always one shot each round that you hit beautifully or takes a lucky bounce that you can puff out your chest and, for a second, think you are Annika Sorenstam or Tiger Woods. I have great memories of golf playing at Shiskine on the Isle of Arran, before going crab fishing, or playing the Old Course at St Andrews – but I feel what I love most is that everyone who has played has their own memories they can access.

Golf has got a range of health benefits – and these are accessible for all.

My Golf Memories

LESLIE (LES) SCHUPAK

The best decision I ever made was bringing my son to my first golf lesson.

I had a late introduction to golf, but it was the catalyst that so dearly has connected our immediate family of now three generations.

At age 35, standing on the lesson tee with my six-year-old son with a cut-down 7-iron in his hand, the two of us started learning how to play, understanding the game's rules, traditions and history, and all of golf's unique components.

Three generations of the Schupak family of golfers

Shortly thereafter, our family went on a holiday trip to La Costa Resort & Spa in Southern California. Again, I found myself standing on the first tee box watching as my now seven-year-old waggled his cut-down Tommy Bolt driver. But what were all the caddies and professional staff milling around watching? When I asked the caddie master, he said, trying to hold back a huge grin, 'There's a bit of wagering going on to see if you can outdrive the young man'.

Not to be left alone at home or on the beach, my wife made the wise decision to become a golfer. Incredibly, all three family members have experienced the joy of scoring a hole-in-one! I won a BMW convertible for mine, but my wife was a day late and a dollar short in her achievement as there had been a $1 million prize to anyone purchasing a raffle ticket who performed such a feat the previous day!

Experiences multiplied as we all grew older. He and I won our first parent-child championship; then after college graduation, he hoisted the crystal trophy at the first-flight club championship at TPC Sawgrass, and not long ago we teamed to triumph against a hundred media members at the Tour Edge Media Invitational in Orlando.

Mom did equally well. She was crowned the President's Cup winner at Metropolis Country Club in White Plains, NY, where she and her partner were underdogs against 72 other competitive women. She was on a roll when shortly thereafter that triumph, she knocked in that ace at the renowned Grossingers Country Club golf course in the Catskill Mountains region of New York.

My son, Adam, grew up to become a prize-winning golf writer and author, following in the footsteps of his father. While building his career, he met a woman who would become his wife and the family's best golfer. They met at the Arnold Palmer Invitational – thanks Arnold – and she has carved her own path in the golf industry after playing competitively at Wake Forest University. Together they won the Jacksonville Area Golf Association Couples Division championship over a stellar field.

However, the best prize arrived in March 2021 when the couple presented the family's third generation, a daughter enriched with a substantial portion of golf DNA. To prove that, prior to her first birthday, standing on a practice putting green, she picked up a golf ball, strode to the nearest hole, and placed it therein. As cheers and applause surrounded her, she gave a big smile and clapped her hands.

It was just another reminder of how much this great game has given us. To which we all say, 'Thank you golf. What memories you have given our family'.

The 16th, Old Tom's Pulpit

for R P MacDonald

MORAG ANDERSON

The northern ice sheet retreats,
slowly exposes coastal shelves
that stretch the length of Askernish.
Atlantic swells carve crushed shells.

Cattle shelter in winter hollows,
huddle in nature's bunkers, graze
fairways from summer meadows,
crop sweet buttercups green.

1891, Tom Morris arrives,
surveys the land with an expert eye,
declares the links *second to none*.
Eighteen holes scythed by hand.

World wars bring decline, the course lost
to marram grass for three score and ten,
'til Old Tom's Pulpit is resurrected
and the game resumes. Amen.

Stornoway Golf Course

(*circa* 1900)

DONALD MURRAY

Murdo watched each moment someone raised
a golf club in their fingers. He'd shake his head, complain
about the waste of green space, how his sheep had once
   grazed
in fields now occupied by grown men playing a game
he could not begin to understand. These flapping flags.
Tiny circles dug into the ground.
Balls concealed among blades which once snagged
and fluttered tufts of wool. The constant sound
of whack and whistle accompanying their shots.
Each one stirred a storm within him,
thinking of that flock confined inside his croft
and how they had once gathered in these acres,
sheltering beside the walls of a ruined fold
that once used to stand here,

somewhere near – what these men called –
   the eighteenth hole.

What do you Collect?

JAMES DAVIS

'What do you collect?, I am sometimes asked by golf collecting acquaintances, and I find I have no ready answer. Certainly, cluttered about this office and in drifts on shelves and other crannies throughout the house is clear evidence that, in fact, I do collect stuff. Or, perhaps it collects me as there are items I swear I don't recall inviting in.

Not having a large purse, at least one that can be dedicated to golf purchases, I tend to enjoy small items that are easy to display. I find ball markers to be colourful and pleasant reminders of courses visited and golfing partners. Most of the items on hand were gifted by friends or are associated with a particular golfing memory.

How beautiful memories are and how they inspire us!

A quick glance around shows a lovely modern featherball stamped 'LANE', a Western Golf Association press badge, a shot glass with the MacNabb crest, a print of Crystal Downs Golf Club, and a table-top replica of the first and 18th holes of the Old Course, along with The R&A clubhouse and buildings lining the road – all gifted to me by friends and associates who thought I might enjoy them. That makes them special to me.

The articles, poems and stories in this volume are a sample of the memories we hold dear, all created with our golfing friends and families. Memories and stories buoy us when times are difficult, cheer us with thoughts spent on the course – or in the pubs! – in the company of those special friends.

Books are indispensable companions for enjoying the past. On my own shelves are beloved authors with whom I've spent many a happy hour. Quite a few are from the library of Ralph Livingston III, a close friend now gone these many years. Several of these books still bear yellow **Post-it notes** exactly where he placed them, especially Vardon's *How To Play Golf*. These stickers and the pages they inform offer a poignant insight into his thinking with regard to the proper employment of hickory golf clubs.

No doubt the irascible Ralph meant to argue Vardon's points.

I have a friend who likes to say that she ‹collects memories and experiences›. I'm certain that we all do, beyond our fascination for a particular niche of golf collectibles.

When I consider the many mementoes that have followed me home, I'm grateful for the stories that all of them tell. Each has a depth not readily fathomed by the casual onlooker but will keep me supplied with smiles and memories well beyond the inevitable disbursement of the solid things.

Memories are the things we can 'take with us'.

In the Swing

for Walter Ballantyne

AILEEN BALLANTYNE (NÉE GUTHRIE)

Twae things kept him smilin:
walkin hame fae the bank
iviry day at yin o'clock –
a midday meal pipin hot oan the table –
an Nan there, listenin, laughin sometimes –
then it wis back tae the ledgers, rain ur shine.

The ither wis the hill: a 40-mile view oan the tee
frae the Brig tae the Bass Rock –
nae ledgers oan the hill.

Fir 30 year he balanced iviry book tae the penny,
coonted oot the yays or nays
tae mortgages an loans in the toun.
At 60, the Bank gi'ed him a bress-plated clock,
etched wi aa his years thare.

In retirement, Walter lived oan the hill:
straight as a die he'd hit them,
his een aye oan the sky –
birdies, an eagle even –
only the albatross escaped him.

It's nae aboot the power or the strength, he'd say
it's aboot the swing – even when ye're aulder, weaker,
– the rhythm o the swing niver leaves ye.

The ledgers drew him in still nou and then:
twae skills Walter chose tae gie awaa nou –

yin wis tae the Lifeboat: balancin the books,
coontin pennies, savin lives;

the ither wis the Kirk: coontin the collection,
coontin oot the beat; playin iviry note:
Walter made the organ's
hymns soar yince a month.

But ayeways, ayeways the hill.
It was only when he stoppt gan up the hill at 86,
his feet and legs ower sair nou fir the swing,
that Walter left us, quiet, unassumin,

a gless o watter and his specs,
tidy oan his bedside table,
his slippers bi the bed,

lik he'd just walked oot
fir yin last roond
up the hill.

A Golfer's Tale

GEORGE CONSTABLE

I always liked a laugh on the golf course, that was the main thing. The golf wasn't maybe very good, but you got a good laugh with some of the players you were with.

About 25 years ago, I was playing Camperdown Golf Course, Dundee, with a group of three friends. The 16th fairway backs onto Camperdown Wildlife Centre where the four-legged animals live – horses, zebras and donkeys.

It was a friendly game. Our opponents had won the last hole so teed off first on the 16th. I then played my tee shot. My friend and playing partner, Jim, was quite a character and very astute. He stepped up to the tee and was at the top of his backswing when, all of a sudden, there was a very loud 'Hee-Haw' from the zoo as one of the donkeys started braying, which put Jim off. He sclaffed his shot, the ball just trundling a few feet in front of him.

I was on my knees, howling with laughter, our opponents were having a good laugh about it too. He asked if he could take his shot again but was told, 'No!' Jim took it very well.

Up Glencruitten Golf Course

ANDY BRECKENRIDGE

It's best going out by yourself either
early morning, or much later, maybe
after a day of rain, when new water
hazards mirror the sky and well-trodden
burn crossings suck at your shoes. No walkers
around, no lovers or sheep to rustle
the bronze bracken, or kids hacking about
in the rough, feeling with their soles for lost
Top Flites, Dunlop 65s or Penfold
Commandos. The last train will have just looped
past and round into town. October's good.

Then you might get to see them on the four
holes on the other side of the road, by
the old sawmill. Four or five roe deer walking
slowly, silently along the fourteenth
fairway. The rain hangs on the grass and makes
a white film. You can see their tracks in it.
They'll follow the burn though. There is nothing
to interest them up on the green. Then
they may bear right and head up by MacKay's Pond
if they can get across the railway line.

The quarry blasts bury boulders in the boggy
ground on the eighteenth fairway, sent by
The Major, too in love with dynamite.

It's better on the other side up by
the sawmill, although I did hear the shotgun blast
that removed the brain of the rabbit, slowed
by myxomatosis, near the fifteenth green.

Crazy Happy – Crazy Golf

GABRIELLE BARNBY

Three years old,
Arms aloft,
Claiming the sky
For bright trophy.

Small club
Gripped tight
In toddler plump fist
As dimpled ball whirlpools down.

Odds beaten,
Mum and dad,
Even elder sister,
And the two older brothers.

The youngest,
The blondest,
The one with corrective glasses,
Has done it.

No one else
Could thread
The windmill sails
That turn and turn and turn.

And never stop.

The whole world,
Your exquisite prize,
Your hole in one

Glorious.

You need never play again.

Stunting

GRAHAM FULTON

Whacked dimpled
baby moon ball
bounces on the green
again Monsters
with burnt knees
and backs crash
from rough
alongside terrified clean rodents
They snatch
and drop the ball
into a fat bag
slip secret agently
into bushes
sniggering farting
into short, enormous trousers
with squirming treasure pockets

The golf man wanders puffing puzzled
The train from the sea to Glasgow plods

The monsters pick
stringy fruit pith
from their mouth
urinate briskly
hotly
into bunkers
spit toffee spits
in the pram

pushchair
electric fire
dump
sell the same ball
back to the same man
before it gets
too dark

The tarpaulins groan on the building site
The smokes from the factories wheeze by
There is much left
to look forward to

drunk ramming taxis

vaulting strange
dustcart rust
and tumble dryers

Sergio Garcia trying to find his ball in rough at the 1999 Open, Carnoustie

On the Road

DEBBIE FOLEY

I was a pre-teen in the mid-70s, and my mother and her best friend were single mothers raising kids on their own, three children belonging to my mom and her friend having one daughter. The two energetic single ladies became interested in golf, as my mom tells the story, because taking golf lessons was the best way to meet reputable men. Well, as most kids do, we tagged along to the lessons provided by a golf professional who worked for the city of Elgin, Illinois.

While competitive swimming was my 'main sport', I was intrigued by golf. We lived in a townhouse complex called Garden Quarter Homes, which was right next to Wing Park, which, lucky enough for me, had a 9-hole golf course along the perimeter of the playground and the baseball field.

I enjoyed this new sport so much, my mom took me to a sporting goods store on the other side of town and I purchased my first set of golf clubs: Wilson Patty Berg model with a driver, 3-wood, 5-, 7- and 9-irons, a pitching wedge and a putter. The gorgeous golf bag was powder blue in colour to match the golf grips.

I lived close enough to Wing Park, so I rode my bike, at first with my bag thrown awkwardly over my shoulder, and later by holding the pull cart in one hand and steering my bike with the other. The golf course was a plain layout without water or bunkers, just the road that paralleled the right side of the first fairway and a neighbourhood along the fairways of holes three and four; the rest of the park on the other side of the fence bordered the remaining holes. I wonder how many golf balls I lost as I tried to perfect my swing. Still trying to perfect my swing! The cost to play was just a few dollars so we were able to play all summer long. When my brother played, he would hit a bad shot and simply break the shaft over his knee. I used to think, 'Oh my gosh, we don't have any money to replace his clubs!'. Little did I know that we only needed to replace the shaft, not the whole club.

A few years later, my mother did actually meet and marry a PGA golf professional and I was provided with an avenue to continue playing golf and receive lessons from my stepfather. I eventually went to work for him at a golf course in the suburbs of Ft Lauderdale, Florida: The TPC at Eagle Trace in Coral Springs, then host of the PGA Tour's HONDA CLASSIC. I had the honour of working for the TPC Network for ten years before going to work for the PGA of America for the last 23 years, educating aspiring young golf professionals earning PGA Membership. I have met famous golfers including Byron Nelson, Lexi Thompson, Payne Stewart, Nancy Lopez and so many other idols of my youth. I have played numerous golf course in the United States, Germany, Scotland (including the Jubilee Course at St Andrews, Gleneagles and the Ailsa Course at Turnberry), Canada and Santiago, Chile. I've been to spectator events including the PGA Championship, the Ryder Cup, the LPGA's Solheim Cup and numerous PGA Tour events at prestigious golf courses across the country and still my favourite golf course is that little 9-hole track at Wing Park, which now has the honour of being on the National List of Historic Properties. Designed by Thomas Bendelow of Aberdeen, Scotland, the course is one of his 600+ American designs. It has been providing town residents a new opportunity of sport since 1908.

The business and sport of golf has allowed me to develop relationships with thousands of golfers and golf professionals. One special memory includes a few special rounds of golf with Alice Dye, as she was an Independent Director for the PGA of America in the early 2000s. My special memory of Alice was when she invited me to play at her home course in Florida and then return to her house to watch the final round, of all tournaments, the HONDA CLASSIC. So many extraordinary and sometimes surreal moments that will long stay in my memory.

A Poem from Coronaworld, May 2020

GRAHAM FULTON

on the municipal golf course
I swish my sodden shoes
through the long rough
looking for balls
like I did
when I was a kid

I find one which
is hollow and cracked
flooded with gunk

Noodle brand
not made in China

I also discover
a *Wagon Wheels* wrapper
and a red flag on a pole
lying at the fringe
of an island of trees

the cups on the greens
are full of brown water
which could be drunk
in the event
of an emergency

It feels strange
straying so far
I'm waiting for a loudspeaker
from nowhere
asking me what
I think I'm doing

I'm looking for golf balls
is what I will say
just before they take me away

Carnoustie Craws Junior Golf Academy

Members of the Carnoustie Craws with Sergio Garcia (L) and Rory McIlroy (R)

Carnoustie Craws Junior Golf Academy

POETRY COMPETITION ENTRIES

There was two kids from the Craws
Who lost a lot of golf baws
Then they hit the ball straight
It landed on the eighth
And now they think they are great

by Fraser and Hannah Macdonald

There once was a boy called Hunter
Who always hit the golf ball in the bunker
He practised on the Burnside in the sun
Then he eventually got a hole in one

by Fraser and Hannah Macdonald

When I was two and just a wee boy
My grandad bought me a nice new toy.
It wasn't something I'd asked for at all –
A plastic golf club and a white rubber ball!
Then came REAL clubs, a set just for me.
I'd practise all day until Mum shouted "Tea!"
So out in the garden, I gave them a bash.
Dad even thought the windows might SMASH!
Any chance we had, we were on the green,

Me and my grandad, the happiest we'd been.
Up at the Nestie, we could stay there all day.
We'd hit great shots and laugh as we play.
Some people think Rory is surely the best
But there's one golfer for me above all the rest.
He's nice and he's kind, the best teacher I've had
And that's why he's my awesome grandad.

by Lucas Mannion

Brody's Grandad

I'm 8 years old but truth be told, it seems a whole lot more.
The tales about my grandad
and about him shouting fore.
Whether on the Burnside or the Buddon, it doesn't really matter.
His art of finding water, will never cease to flatter.

He found it on the right side,
he has found it on the left.
He even found the water
whilst putting on the twelfth.
When we get the chance to head out on the links
It really makes me glad.
Because there is no better way to spend the day
than golfing with my grandad.

by Brody Macfarlane

There was a man who liked to swing a golf club,
And he also liked to eat a lot of grub,
He hit the ball towards the hole but it was stolen by a mole,
So he gave up and instead headed to the pub.

by Sophie Yu

Nestie Any Time!

On a warm summer's day
Or a cold winters eve
Put on my cap and grab my clubs
Run to the Nestie,
To hole some putts

by Owen Thomson

On the links there's a man called Rod Soutar,
Who frequently fluffs a 2-footer,
He's never off the range, which I find very strange,
He probably needs a new tutor.

by Gordon Harris (parent)

There once was a golfer named Keir,
Whose stroke looked very queer,
When he took a swing
With his favourite Ping,
His rivals, him they did fear!

by Nigel Robinson (parent)

There once was a lass,
Who played golf with some sass,
She wasn't at all nerdy,
When she got a birdie,
Chipping in from the long grass.

by Nigel Robinson (parent)

ACE

I want to be as good as the cool guyz
With a stroke that will take you by surprise
Sink a hole in one, that will be lots of fun
And be up there with McIlroy, Fleetwood and Crean

by Lachlan Johnston

Bill Murray

My favourite golfer is Bill Murray
I see him at the Dunhill Links and he's really really funny
He doesn't take his time; he's always in a hurry
He might miss a putt or two but he never seems to
   worry
Who ya gonna call? The Golf-Buster!

by Owen Thomson and Grandad

The Fifth Major in Golf

MICHAEL WHITE

Every golf fan can rattle off the names of the four Major trophies and many of their past winners. What about the holder of the fifth Major, or should that be retitled the fifth major achievement?

Let me take you back to the year 2015 and an invitation to attend an 'event' in the little village of Hightae, near Lockerbie in Dumfries and Galloway. The locally based activities co-ordinator with Alzheimer Scotland had been a great supporter of Golf Memories and had taken up an offer from her neighbour to stage The Hightae Open. She was ably supported by a group of volunteers from Dumfries and Galloway Golf Club, who had been instrumental in setting up a Golf Memories group at their own club.

I was amazed to see what they had organised. The neighbour had quite an extensive garden but had struck a 'deal' with a local farmer to get access to another strip of land beyond his own perimeter fence, provided he let the farmer's sheep have grazing rights on the 'course' when not in use.

A course had been constructed with an amazing network of criss-cross holes and cuts of the lawn had made quite impressive greens. The addition of flags and hospitality tents gave a surreal feel to the day, but that paled into insignificance when the players arrived. Nearly all of them were living with dementia and some had quite serious mobility issues. What they had in common was a passion for the sport they loved – golf.

It was to prove a most humbling and eye-opening experience for me and confirmed my thinking that through reminiscence and linked physical activity, much can be done to improve the lives of those who are living with dementia and other memory problems.

Bill (not his real name) was one of the first to arrive and he was duly supported by his carer as he shuffled across the lawn to take his seat and enjoy a cup of coffee. His blazer badge was a clue as to his military experience, and we duly chatted away about his distinguished career in the RAF. It would be fair to say that Bill was struggling with his movement and looked distinctly unsteady on his feet. He seemed quite at ease watching the others putting and practising drives, but we could sense that he was growing slightly restless. He astounded everyone by asking if he could 'have a shot'.

Bill

Thoughts of impending medical emergencies, litigation and court appearances flashed through my head, as he struggled to get out of his chair, even though he was properly supported by his carer and a volunteer. He shuffled down to what was to be the 1st tee, and even making the 20-yard journey was a considerable achievement. He swayed slightly and again I feared the worst. He was given a 5-iron and examined the club. What happened next was simply bewildering, amazing and, I must confess, left all of us with a tear in the eye.

All kinds of past experiences must have been dragged out of his memory banks as we watched a remarkable transformation in front of our eyes.

From a stooped, shuffling old man he gradually stood erect and steadied himself. We all held our breath as he took two or three practice swings, and to be honest the fact that he hadn't fallen over was an achievement. He gave a swing of his hips and eyed up the intended target. There was a problem directly ahead – the neighbour's wooden fence; a good shot would be needed to clear it.

The carer stood behind him, ready to dive in and rescue the situation but Bill was perfectly steady and ready for action.

He looked at his ball. Then the fence. Then the distant hole. I couldn't believe what I was witnessing. Bill was throwing off the years and the associated problems of age-related mobility. He addressed his ball and hit a shot which cleared the fence with ease and headed down the makeshift fairway. The smile said it all. The applause from all those who were there was loud and sincere. It was utterly amazing to have seen this.

Bill's transformation was short lived, and he soon reverted to his previously-observed state. Aided by his carer, he shuffled back to the chair and enjoyed the rest of the day. He must have been a good golfer in his day and the motor memory was still there once the club was placed in his hand. How many more *former* golfers could become golfers again and find support and therapy by picking up a club, joining a Golf Memories group and taking part in the game they loved – and still do?

Bill's major achievement was to be the inspiration for Golf Memories at other clubs.

Cherishing Memories

RICHARD McBREARTY

Intro

Communities across Scotland, and indeed around the world, have always met together to share experiences. These meetings may be held by chance in local venues and shops, or by design in libraries, reminiscence groups or sports and social clubs. We value and cherish these interactions. For many, they are amongst the most important aspects of life. We may place a value on our things, our possessions and even achievements, but our memories are sacred and irreplaceable. To share these with friends, old and new, is a wonderful way to connect. For those living with dementia, memories, often long-term ones, can be triggered and enjoyed by interactions, stimulus and discussions with those around them.

We are stronger together than we are alone. And upon this principle, the various memories projects in Scotland were built.

People to People

Memories Scotland is the extension of Scotland-wide projects connecting heritage resources with reminiscence activity across sectors and themes. It has evolved from the growth in, and consistent need for, locally led community connections, even during the global pandemic.

The Foundations

In 2009, Football Memories Scotland was launched, an innovative national extension of a local project which was supported by members of the Scottish Football Heritage Network, managed by the Scottish Football Museum and funded by Alzheimer Scotland.

Specially trained volunteers were equipped with access to a rich archive of digital images of footballing history and they organised football reminiscence groups around the country, focusing on being dementia-friendly and supporting those living with dementia and other memory problems.

Making an Impact

Groups began to meet regularly to share their football memories and following a successful one-year pilot, the project was evaluated and then established as the world's first national football reminiscence programme. As this impact has developed over the years, so has the project's reach. Over 360 groups now meet regularly in community settings, sports grounds, hospitals and care homes around the country to discuss their favourite footballing memories, and much more into the bargain. Physical activity has been linked through the Walking Football initiative. The same principles were applied to a range of other sports. These groups meet in a variety of settings, especially golf, shinty and rugby clubs. Cricket and speedway groups have also developed. The sports-based archive was extended during a successful pilot programme as Sports Heritage Scotland. Golf Memories has developed to include golf-related physical activities and has been incredibly successful. It is hoped that the other sports will do likewise, as the combination of golf-based reminiscence activity with related physical engagement has been effective and, at times, spectacular.

Moving Forward and Joining Forces

In 2021, the archive was relaunched as Memories Scotland. Building on the existing infrastructure and initial experiences of the Football Memories project, Memories Scotland is the result of a partnership with Scottish libraries, supported by the Scottish Government's Public Library Improvement Fund, and administered by the Scottish Library and Information Council. Its aim is to work collaboratively with Golf Memories Scotland, which was established in 2015, to support their planned programme of expanding and increasing the reach of the Golf Memories groups across Scotland. In addition, it aims to increase its resource and archive base to meet the recognised growing need for other themed reminiscence groups.

National Reach
The majority of Scotland's regional library services have signed up to the project, sharing social history resources from their local studies collections and working to develop memory groups within their venues.

The project is managed by a steering group under the leadership of North Ayrshire Libraries, with representation from East Dunbartonshire Leisure and Culture Trust, Falkirk Council, Glasgow Life, South Ayrshire Libraries and South Lanarkshire Leisure and Culture Trust as well as the National Library of Scotland and both the chair and Football Memories lead of the Scottish Football Museum. A library development officer is working with library partners to coordinate their contributions to the archive and plan for the roll-out of new memory groups.

R&A World Golf Museum

HANNAH FLEMING

The R&A World Golf Museum and the Royal and Ancient Clubhouse

'I can't believe I'm here' is a refrain we hear regularly from our visitors. Being in St Andrews, next to the Old Course, we are reminded every day what a pilgrimage it is for golfers to see these historic links. We aim to celebrate the past, present and future of golf in our collections, displays and events, and are honoured to be involved with Golf Memories Scotland.

Memories are embedded in the work we do, and I have learned what a positive effect a reminiscence session can achieve. Holding a golf club again after a period of illness, looking through a treasured Open programme, or watching Seve joyfully celebrate his winning moment, can be transformative for the person living with dementia. As facilitator for the group, my day is enriched when I learn more by speaking and listening to golf enthusiasts. Their stories and memories bring personal insights to moments of history, deepening my own understanding of our sport.

Discussions can meander between topics, but we use our museum objects and imagery as the teeing off point to uncover hidden memories. The feelings attached to golf linger in the person who is no longer able to compete on the course. Positive associations of friendship, travel and the excitement of being part of a crowd, even flashes of frustration at golf shots gone wrong, are sympathetically welcomed by the group.

Living with dementia (or being a carer for someone with dementia) can feel isolating, upsetting and feeling out of step with the world. For a brief time, even an hour or so, they can have a connection with a favourite activity when positive associations come flooding back, thus lifting the spirits of all involved. The moment when someone with dementia recollects how it felt to watch a favourite player lift a trophy, a joy is brought to their face and that can be priceless, and a privilege to witness.

Golf Memories

Reconnecting people with their passion for golf as players or spectators

The key aim of Golf Memories is to reconnect people with the 'golf family and community', to rekindle a love of the game, share memories and create new special memories for them and their loved ones.

Golf Memories groups are all volunteer-led and bring together golf enthusiasts who, like the members, love to talk, share and participate in everything golf related. Those attending come from a variety of backgrounds, but they come together as golf fans.

The memories of their playing days are immensely powerful and for those who now have a problem with recalling recent events, these specific memories are still there. Golf Memories aims to capture these memories for future interest, to be used as a rich resource of oral history. People living with dementia can provide first-hand accounts of important parts of social and economic history, especially cultural aspects.

The images used in the sessions depend very much upon the age of the person but will usually focus on the period when they were children, teenagers and younger adults. The often-amazing level of recall that is experienced affords younger family members and friends an almost encyclopaedic insight into their loved one's younger years.

As of 2022, the period covered in Golf Memories' sessions is 1945–2000, although some older members talk about playing golf in the pre-war years with remarkable clarity. Although the images used in sessions are primarily photographs, increased use is being made of short video clips.

When Golf Memories started its journey, it quickly became aware of the remarkable benefits attached to physical activity and golf. The positive impact of holding a golf club once again, putting or using simulation bays was incredible. Golf Memories has been honoured to witness countless examples of individuals reverting some 40 years when they once again hold a golf club in their hands.

Feedback from family members and friends has been and still is a powerful testament to the benefits of Golf Memories and specifically to the benefits of physical activity and golf.

Golf Memories: Member, Carer and Family Commendations

"The aim and positive outcome of Golf Memories extends beyond the needs of those who attend the sessions to those who love and care for them. These are some of their comments."

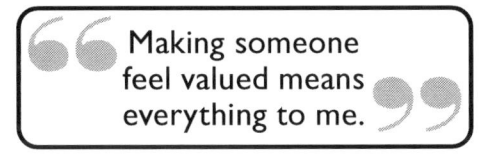

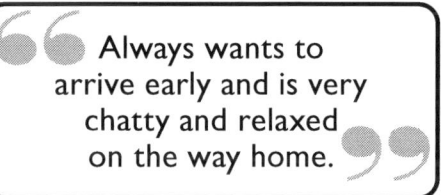

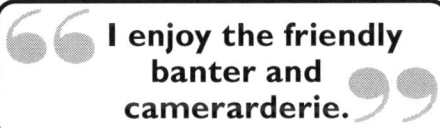

> Making someone feel valued means everything to me.

> Always wants to arrive early and is very chatty and relaxed on the way home.

> **I enjoy the friendly banter and camerarderie.**

> **BRILLIANT!**

> I really enjoy the golf days. Brings back many happy memories of my playing days and the chance to tell my stories.

> SMILING HAPPY FACES SAY IT ALL!

> My husband really looks forward to the golf group and spending time with his friends.

> After each session I get my dad back – a special feeling.

> He comes prepared for golf and enjoys his time in the simulation bays.

> The visit by Adam Scott was incredibly special. My husband still treasures the photo of himself with Adam.

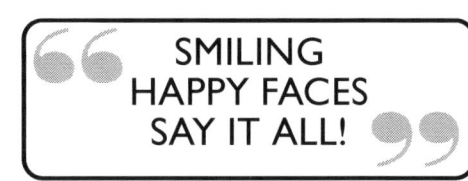

Golf Memories Cards

Memory cards are a useful tool in sports reminiscence therapy. They provide trigger mechanisms for opening discussions and encouraging memory recollection. The laminated cards used by Golf Memories feature, on one side, portraits of golfers who have featured on the world stage over the years as well as those who are not so well-known. The reverse side of the cards offer clues to assist recall by listing honours won by the player and some notable facts about them.

Thanks to the support of The R&A, a new set of cards is being created to celebrate the achievements of the great and good in The Open Championship over the years.

The next section contains 12 Golf Memories cards that collectively provide an insight into the memory cards currently in use.

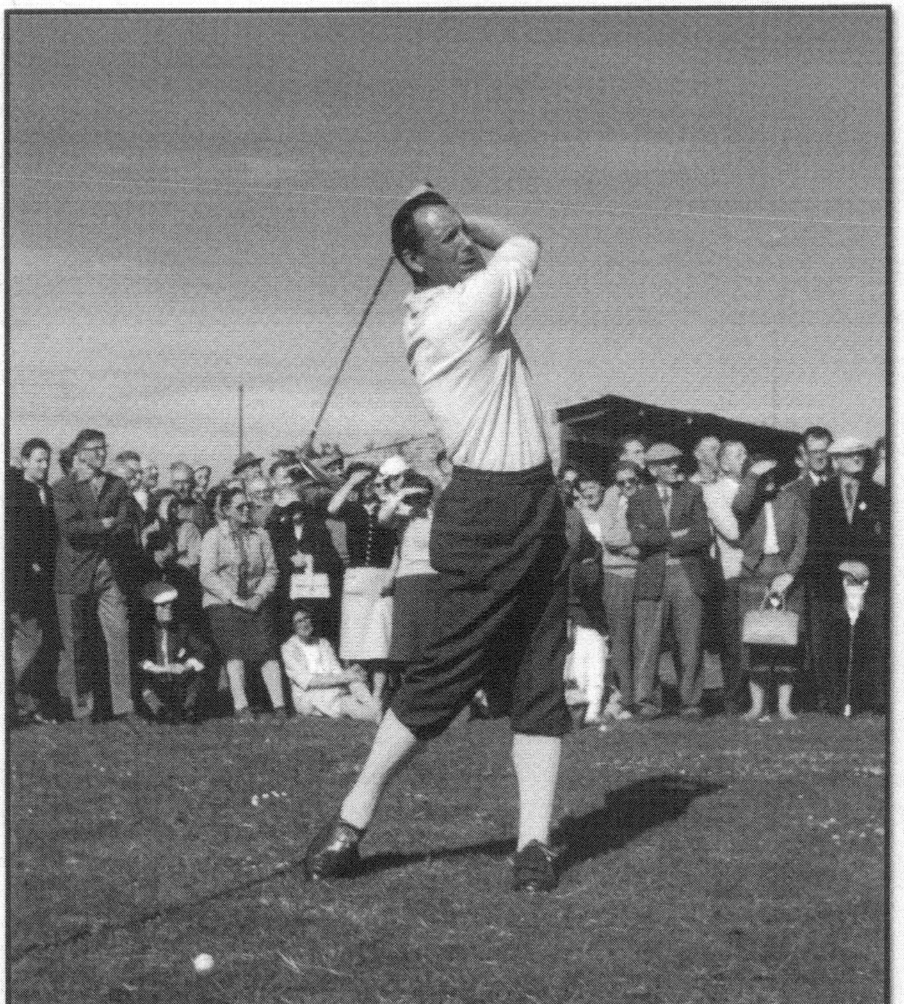

MAX FAULKNER

HONOURS: (Ryder Cup appearances) 1947, 1949, 1951, 1953, 1957, (Major Titles) Open Championship winner 1951

NOTABLE FACTS: Max Faulkner enjoyed a long Open career stretching over 40 years from 1934 to 1975 and would win the famous claret jug at the 1951 Open in Royal Portrush. He dressed in colourful outfits which were quite different to the golf wear of the time and was a flamboyant and extroverted character on the course.

MIND THE LINKS – GOLF MEMORIES

ARNOLD PALMER

HONOURS: (Ryder Cup appearances) 1961, 1963, 1965, 1967, 1971, & 1973, (Major Titles) Open Championship winner 1961 & 1962, US Open winner 1960, US Masters winner 1958, 1960, 1962 & 1964

NOTABLE FACTS: One of golf's greatest personalities, Arnold Palmer was nicknamed "The King" and along with Jack Nicklaus and Gary Player dominated golf during the 1960s. He would win 62 PGA Tour titles during a long and memorable career which included seven major titles.

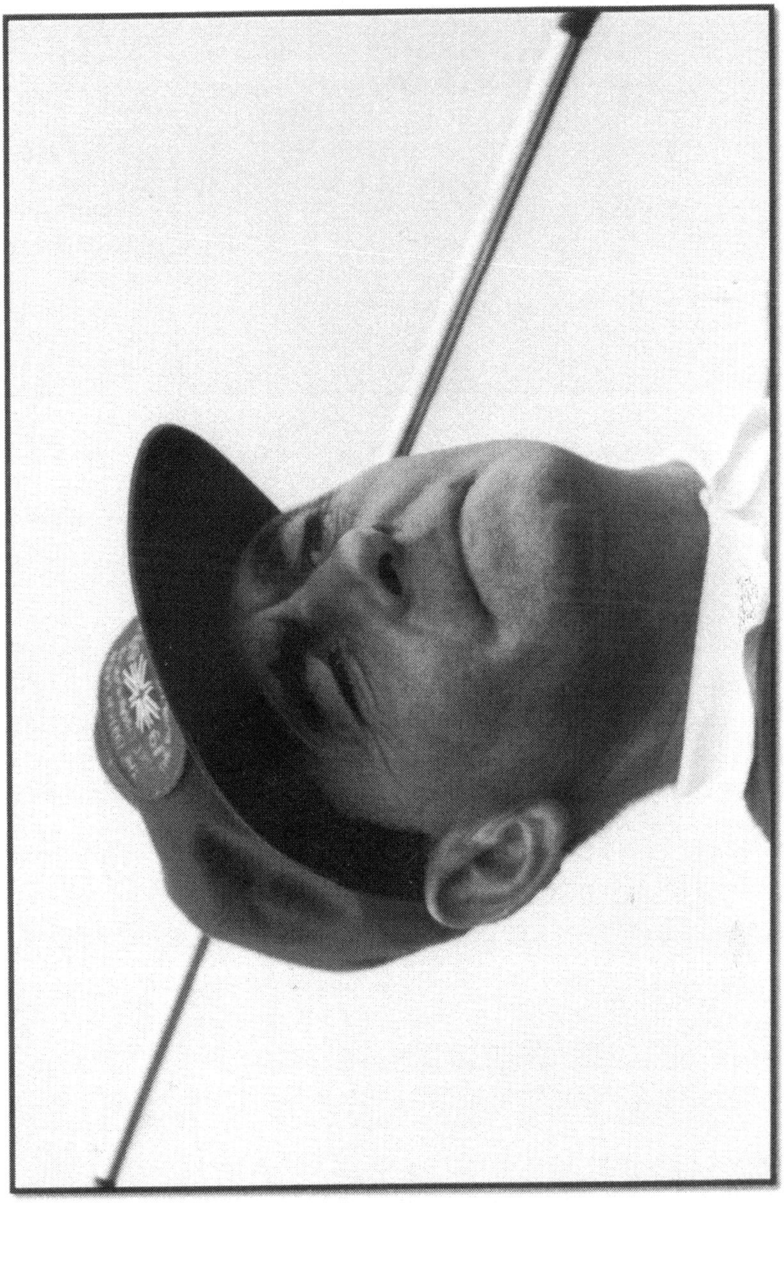

CHRISTIE O'CONNOR

HONOURS: (Ryder Cup appearances) 1955, 1957, 1959, 1961, 1963, 1965, 1967, 1969, 1971 & 1973 (Major Titles) Open Championship runner up 1965

NOTABLE FACTS: One of Ireland's finest golfers, Christie O'Connor Snr had 22 wins on the European circuit including the British Masters in 1956 and 1959 and the John Player Classic in 1970. He played in every Ryder Cup tournament from 1955 to 1973 and his achievement of 10 appearances stood as a record until 1997 when he was finally surpassed by Nick Faldo.

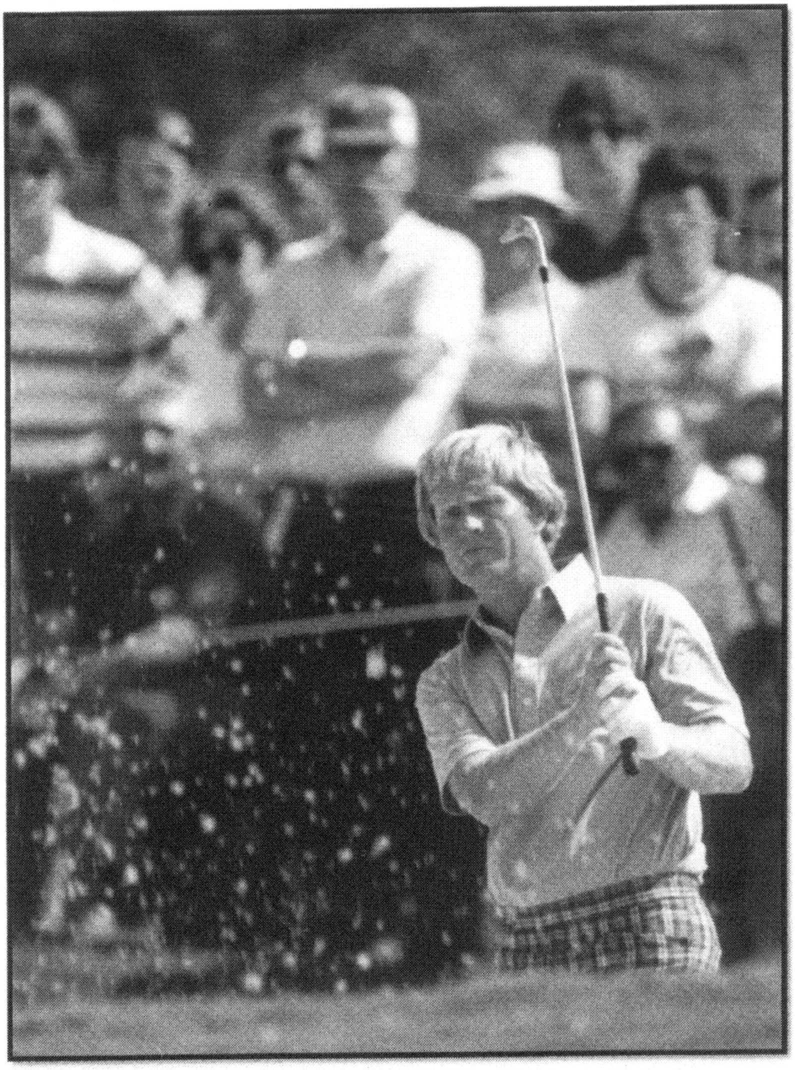

JACK NICKLAUS

HONOURS: (Ryder Cup Appearances), 1969, 1971, 1973, 1975, 1977 & 1981, (Major Titles) Open Championship winner 1966, 1970 & 1978, US Open winner 1962, 1967, 1972 & 1980, US Masters winner 1963, 1965, 1966, 1972, 1975, 1986, PGA Championship winner 1963, 1971, 1973, 1975 & 1980

NOTABLE FACTS: Nicknamed the "Golden Bear", Nicklaus is regarded by many experts to be the greatest golfer of all time. In a career spanning more than a quarter of a century he would win 18 major championships. His final major title came in the US Masters in 1986 and at 46 years of age Nicklaus became the oldest winner of the tournament.

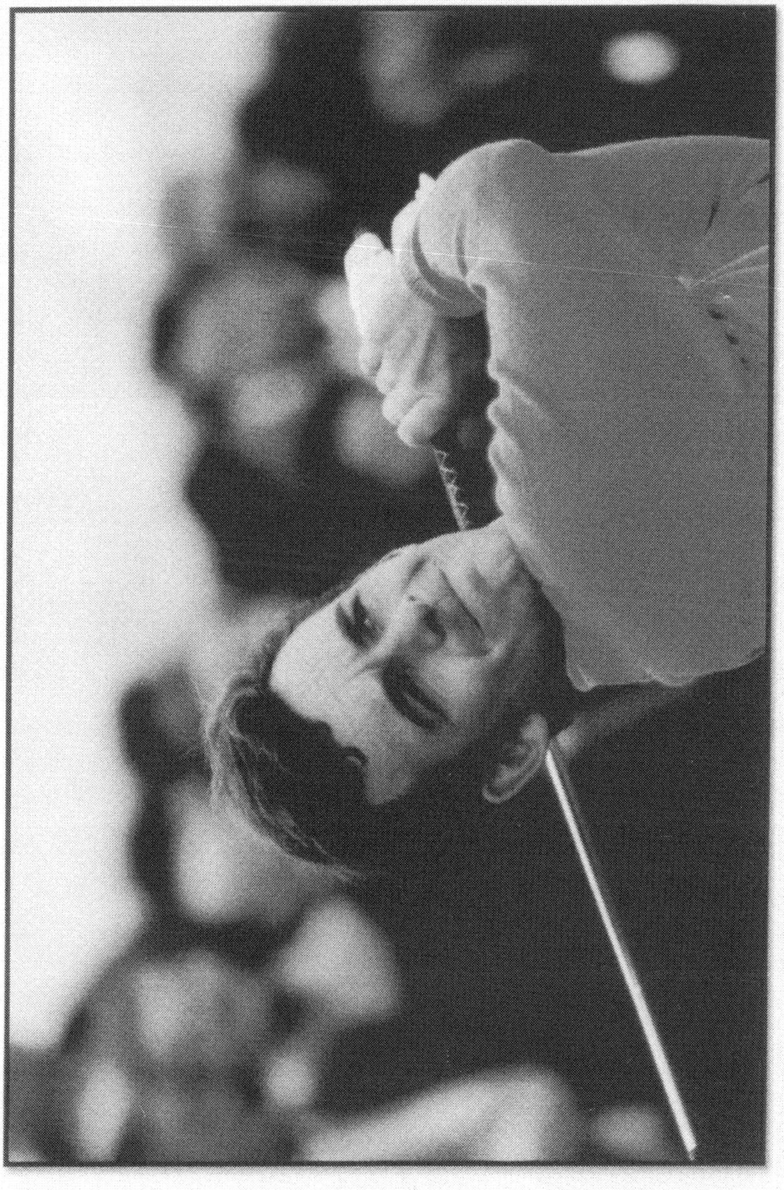

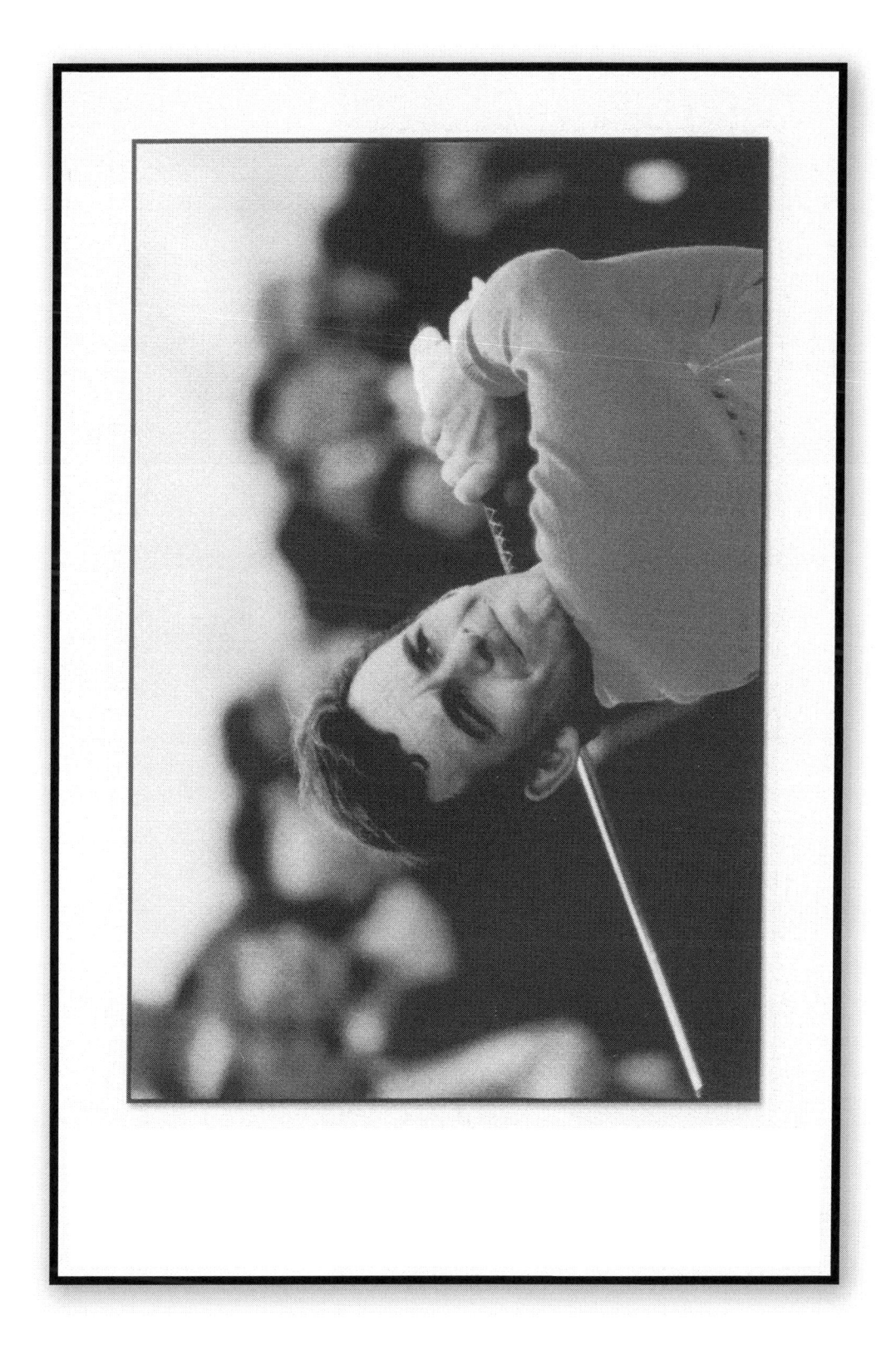

TONY JACKLIN

HONOURS: (Ryder Cup Appearances), 1967, 1969, 1971, 1973, 1975, 1977, 1979 & 1983, (Major Titles) Open Championship winner 1969, US Open 1970

NOTABLE FACTS: The Englishman who is regarded as the finest British player of his generation won the 1969 Open Championship and 1970 US Open, becoming the first British golfer since Harry Vardon to hold both major titles at the same time. Jacklin played at eight Ryder Cups and was non-playing captain for Europe in the tournaments of 1985, 1987 and 1989.

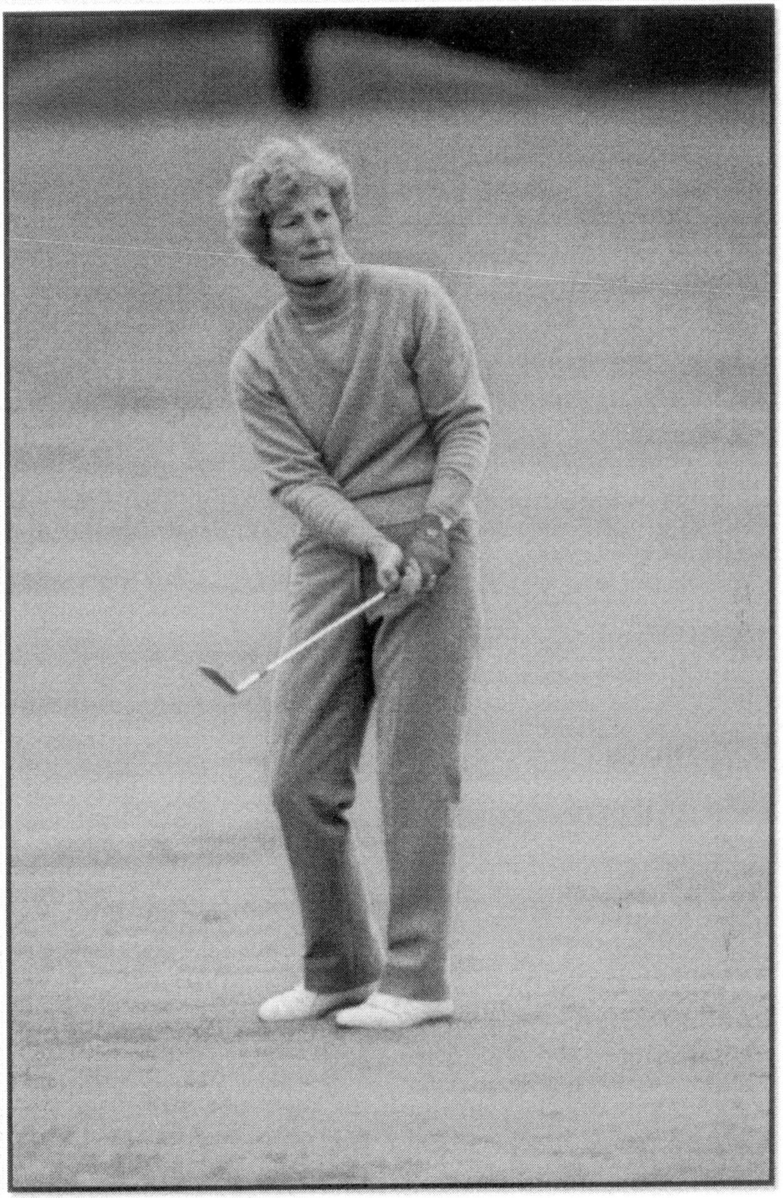

BELLE ROBERTSON

HONOURS: (Curtis Cup appearances) 1960, 1966, 1968, 1970, 1972, 1982 & 1986, (Major Titles) British Ladies Championship winner 1981, Scottish Women's Championship winner 1965, 1966, 1971, 1972, 1978, 1980 & 1986

NOTABLE FACTS: Belle has been voted Scottish Sportswoman of the Year on no less than four occasions. She has represented Great Britain and Ireland nine times in the Curtis Cup, seven as a player and two as a non-playing captain. In 2015 she became one of the first female members of the Royal and Ancient Golf Club of St Andrews.

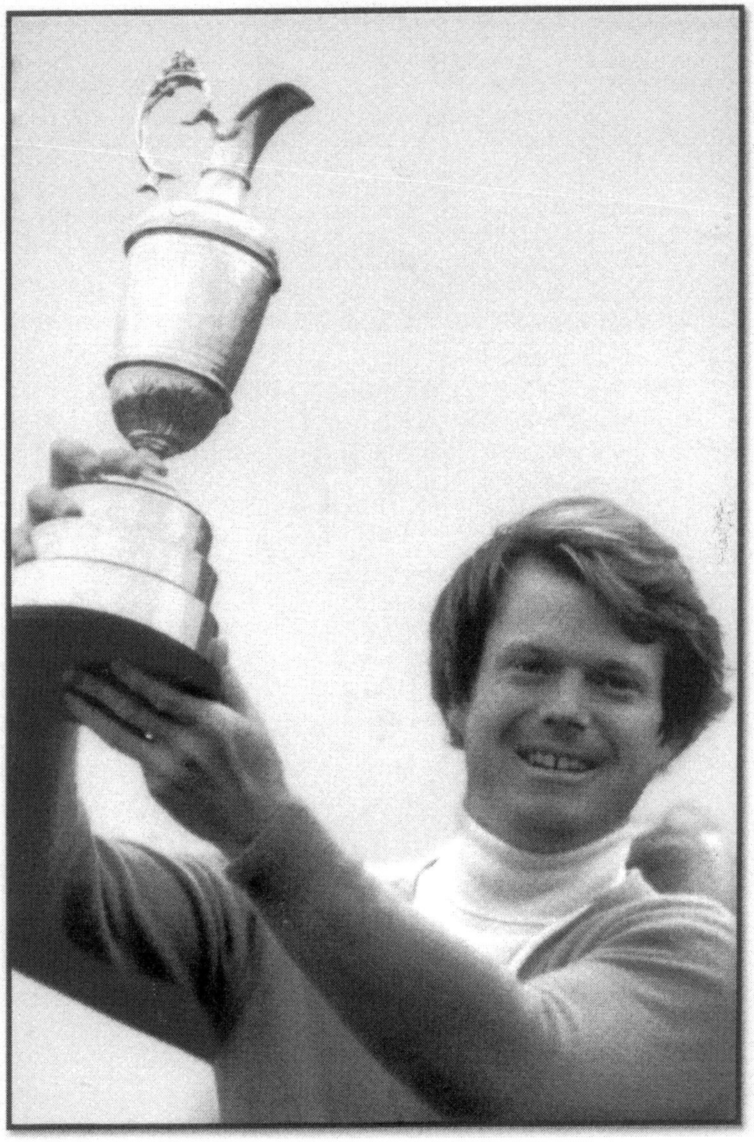

TOM WATSON

HONOURS: (Ryder Cup appearances) 1977, 1981, 1983, & 1989, (Major Titles) Open Championship winner 1975, 1977, 1980, 1982 & 1983, US Open winner 1982, US Masters winner 1977 & 1981

NOTABLE FACTS: Watson was one of the leading players of world golf during the 1970s and 1980s winning eight major titles. Watson's position as one of golf's greatest ever links players can be seen by his success in the Open Championship which he won five times. Having previously won the Open at Turnberry in 1977, he was runner up at the same venue in 2009 when competing at the age of 59.

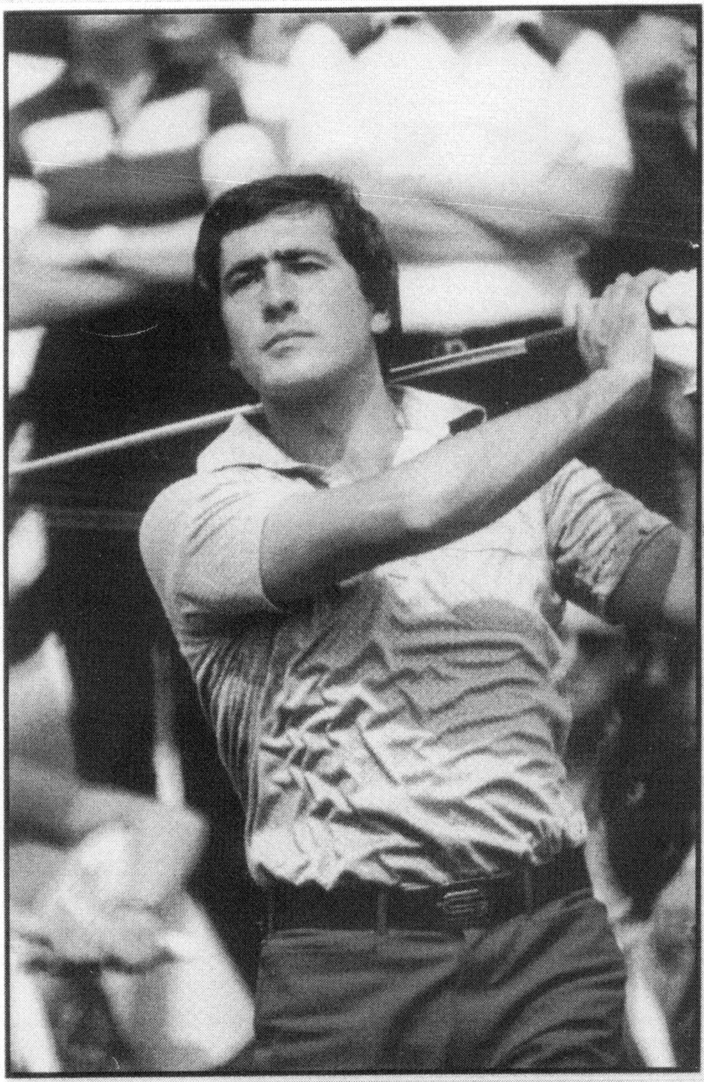

SEVE BALLESTEROS

HONOURS: (Ryder Cup appearances) 1979, 1983, 1985, 1987, 1989, 1991, 1993 & 1995 (Major Titles) Open Championship winner 1979, 1984 & 1988, US Masters winner 1980 & 1983

NOTABLE FACTS: Seve was one of world golf's leading lights for two decades with 91 professional tournament wins, including five major titles. He was a driving force in the emergence of Europe as a successful force in the Ryder Cup, winning five times as a player and captain.

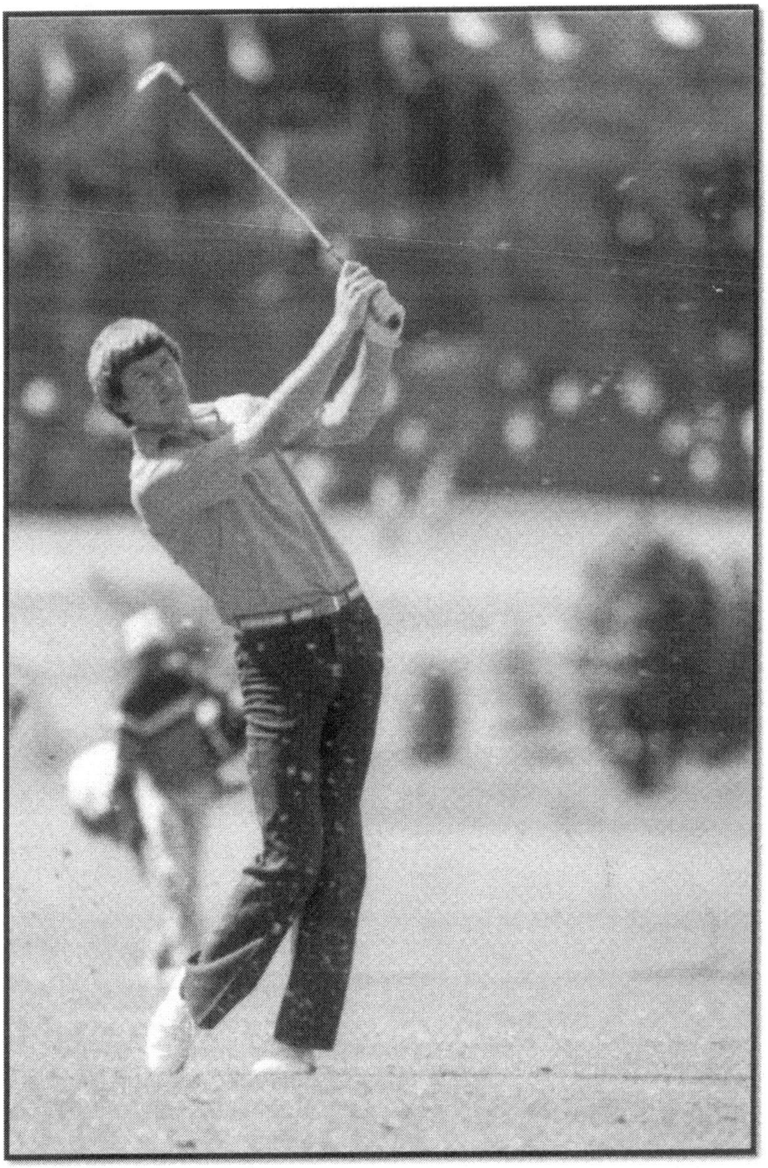

NICK FALDO

HONOURS: (Ryder Cup Appearances) 1977, 1979, 1981, 1983, 1985, 1987, 1989, 1991, 1993, 1995 & 1997, (Major Titles) US Open runner up 1988, Open Championship winner 1987, 1990 & 1992, US Masters winner 1989, 1990 & 1996

NOTABLE FACTS: This English golfer enjoyed a fantastic career with 41 professional wins to his name including three Open Championships and three US Masters victories. He holds the record for most Ryder Cup appearances for Europe (11) and played in his first tournament when just 20 years old. He was PGA Player of the Year in 1990 and European Tour Player of the Year in 1989, 1990 and 1992.

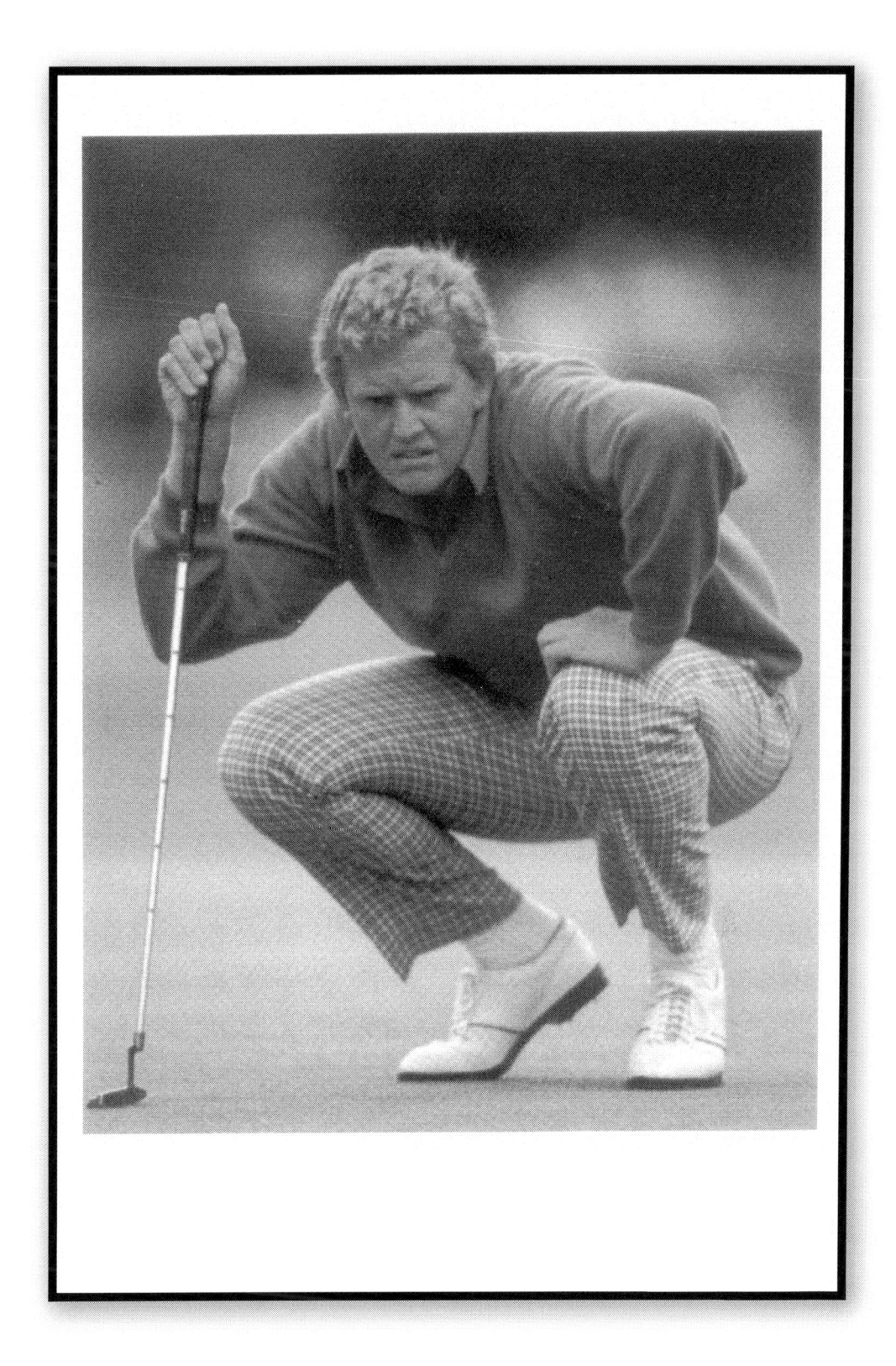

COLIN MONTGOMERIE

HONOURS: (Ryder Cup appearances) 1991, 1993, 1995, 1997, 1999, 2002, 2004 & 2006 (Major Titles) Open Championship runner up 2005, US Open runner up 1994, 1997 & 2006, PGA Championship runner up 1995

NOTABLE FACTS: "Monty" won 31 European Tour events and never lost a singles match in eight Ryder Cup appearances. He has won a record eight European Order of Merit titles, including a run of seven consecutively from 1993 to 1999.

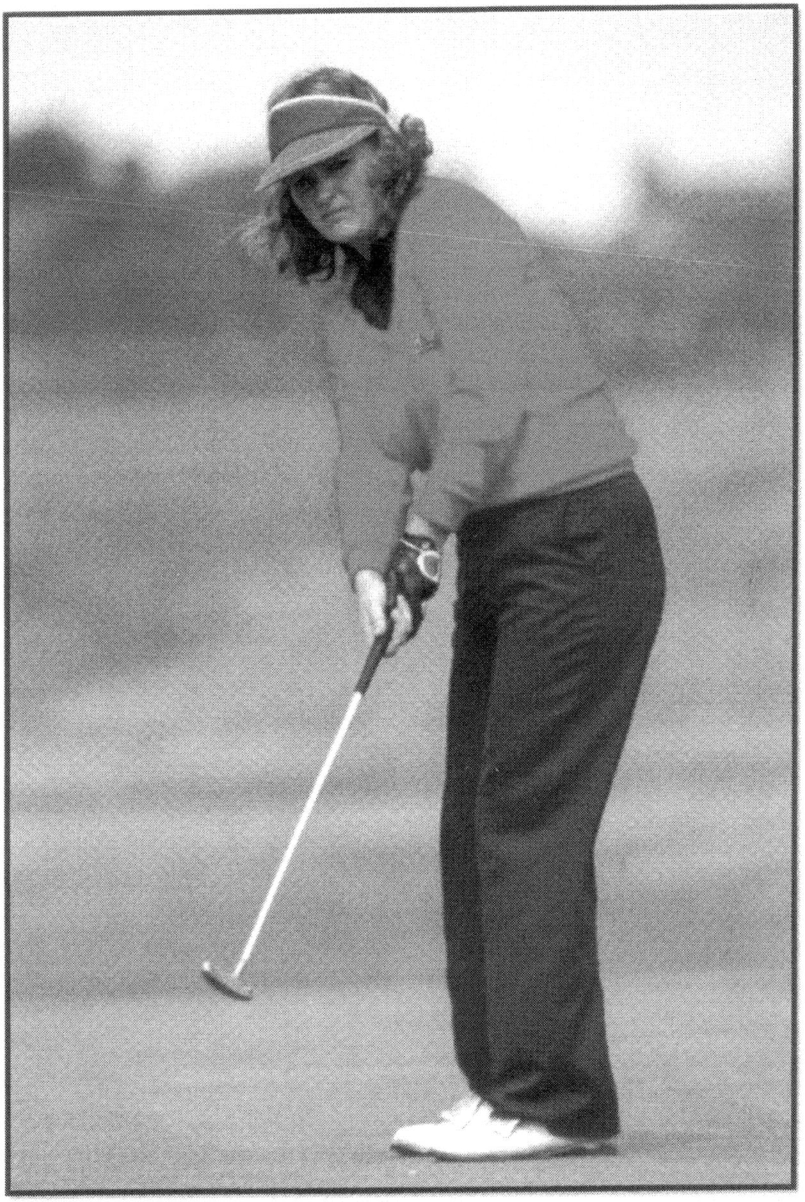

CATHY PANTON-LEWIS

HONOURS: (Major Titles) British Ladies Championship winner 1976, Irish Ladies' Open 1983, Portuguese Ladies' Open 1986 & 1987

NOTABLE FACTS: Catherine Panton-Lewis was a founding member of the Ladies European Tour and won its first Order of Merit in 1979. In 1976 she won the British Ladies' Amateur Championship, was named Scottish Sportswoman of the Year and turned professional. She went on to win 14 tournaments on the Ladies European Tour.

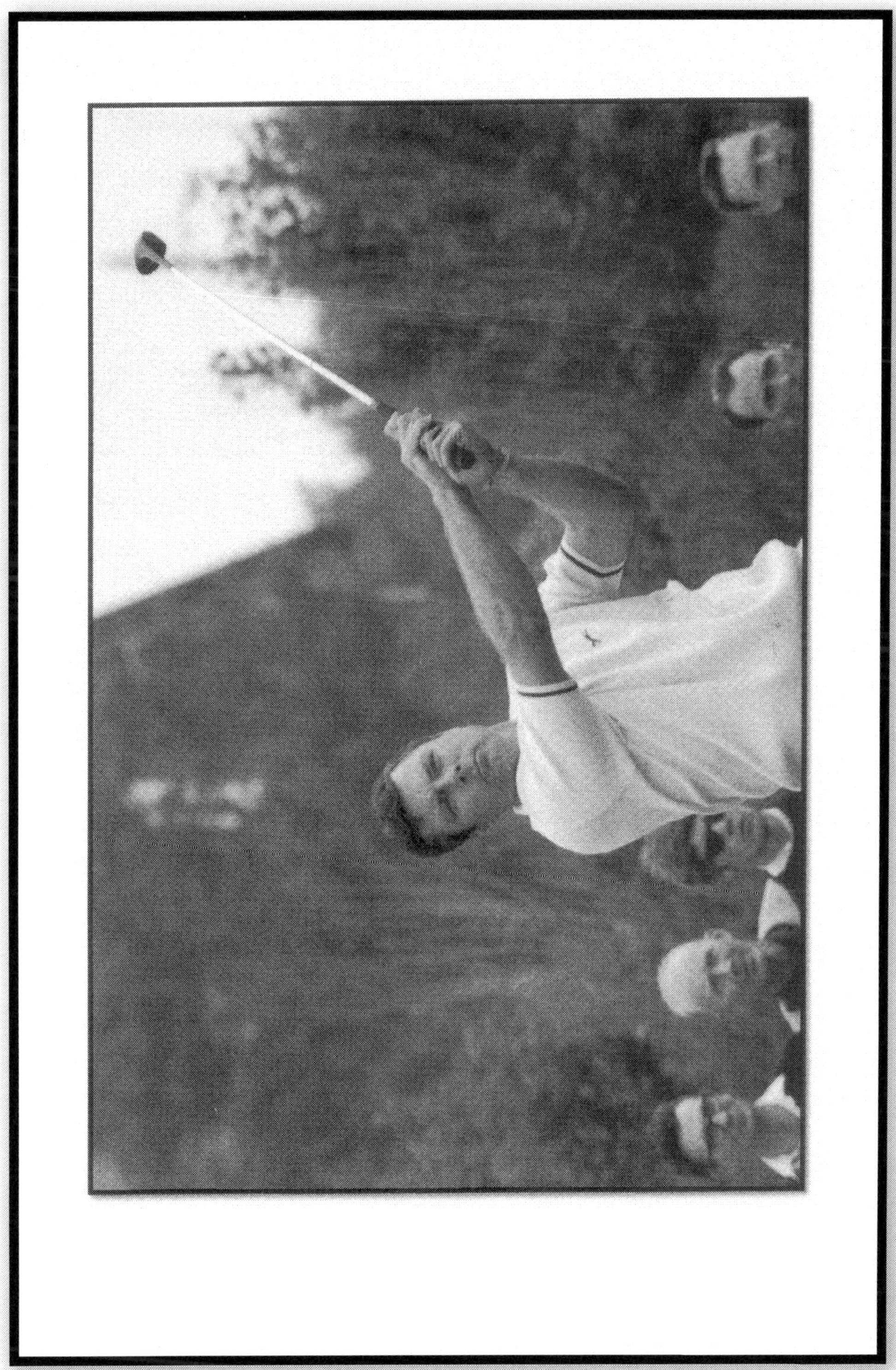

PETER ALLISS

HONOURS: (Ryder Cup appearances) 1953, 1957, 1959, 1961, 1963, 1965, 1967 & 1969

NOTABLE FACTS: Alliss enjoyed 31 professional wins in a memorable and successful career which included three British PGA Championship titles and eight selections for Great Britain & Ireland in the Ryder Cup between 1953 and 1969. Commonly known as the "Voice of Golf" for his television commentary, Peter and his father Percy were the first father and son to both play in the Ryder Cup.

Tom Watson, Carnoustie

Postscript

Links Song

W G STRACHAN
**First published in *College Echoes*, XXII,
9 December 1910**

When the ultimate 'Fore' has been shouted
And the Swilcan is baked and dried,
When the uttermost divot has hurtled
And the youngest caddie has died,
We shall go for a change and we'll need it,
And golf for an aeon or so
On the links of the Red Hot Razors
Where all good golfers go.

Round the Course of the Molten Bunkers,
By the sea of the Scorching Squalls
We shall drive with the fireproof Dreadnoughts
And smite the asbestos balls
To the greens of Never Never,
Where the flags are flapping red,
And we'll swear by – the land of the living
When we lay our approaches dead.

For the things we've said to our caddies,
For the things we've said to the ball,
For the things we've said in the bunker
For silence profaner than all,
We shall pay for them each twice over
And again and again and again,
Puffing and panting, perspiring
For ever and ever – Amen.

About the Contributors
THE AFICIONADOS OF GOLF

Morag Anderson is a Scottish poet based in Highland Perthshire. Her debut chapbook, *Sin Is Due to Open in a Room Above Kitty's*, was published in 2021. Her collaborative chapbook, *How Bright the Wings Drive Us*, won the Dreich Alliance Competition in 2021. She was placed in the Oxford Brookes International Poetry Competition, the Edwin Morgan Trust Poetry Competition, and shortlisted for the Bridport Poetry Prize, all in 2021. She has been widely published and anthologised. As one of The Trysting Thorns, she has completed commissions for the Scottish Poetry Library.

Aileen Ballantyne is an award-winning national newspaper journalist turned poet, and the former staff medical correspondent for both *The Guardian* and *The Sunday Times*. Her investigative journalism for *The Guardian* has twice been commended at the British Press Awards. Her first poetry collection, *Taking Flight*, explores flight in all its aspects – including a sequence of poems on Lockerbie, Pan Am flight 103 in the voices of those affected. Her poetry has won a series of major awards including first prize in the prestigious Mslexia Poetry Prize and a Scottish Book Trust New Writers Poetry Award. She has a PhD in Creative Writing and Modern Poetry from the University of Edinburgh. She was born and brought up in Cowdenbeath in Fife and was recently nominated as one of 14 new poets to be included in the Scottish Poetry Library's online guide to notable poets.

Dan Barlow is a visitor services assistant with the National Trust for Scotland.

Gabrielle Barnby lives in Orkney where she writes novels, short stories and poetry. Her work has been included in numerous anthologies, magazines and online. She facilitates creative writing groups in the community with participants aged from eight to 80 and has a strong interest in writing for wellbeing.

David Blair was born and bred in Carnoustie. He was educated at Carnoustie Primary and Arbroath High School. Straight out of high school his working life began in 1950 with DC Thomson's in Dundee where he was employed in editorial work for boys' comics such as *The Hotspur, Wizard, Warlord* and *Victor*. He remained with DC Thomson throughout his working life, retiring in 1986. During his retirement years, he kept himself busy as editor of the monthly magazine for Carnoustie Church and engaged in new interests such as bowls. Golf has always been his first love though; he has held a season ticket for the golf courses since he was 7 or 8 and has been a member of Carnoustie Golf Club for more than 75 years.

Andy Breckenridge is an English teacher living in Brighton but originally from Oban. He writes about self-imposed exile, place, relationships and memory, and his poems often include fish and water. His pamphlet, *The Liquid Air,* was published in July 2021. He has work in several print and online journals and has a full collection *The Twenty Four Hour Water Clock* looking for a home; as well as a second with the working title *The Fish Inside,* which he is currently filleting. He has been a featured writer on Eat The Storms, Flight of the Dragonfly Spoken Word, and reads regularly at the Northern Poets Society.

Michael Breed is one of the most dynamic, engaging and entertaining teachers in the game. He is the host of *Course Record with Michael Breed,* which airs on CBS prior to coverage of the PGA Tour and on CBS Sports Network. He also hosts

A New Breed of Golf on Sirius XM PGA Tour Radio and the digital series *A New Breed of Golf*. He previously hosted the highest-rated golf instruction series for Golf Channel, *The Golf Fix*. He is a member of the PGA of America and contributes to their digital broadcast of the PGA Championship and Ryder Cup. He further serves as Chief Digital Instructor for *Golf Digest*, focused on innovating golf instruction and overseeing the 'Best Young Teachers' program.

Carnoustie Craws Junior Golf Academy, established in 2018, provides young people in the local Carnoustie community with an opportunity to learn and fall in love with golf. With over 350 junior golfers participating in the weekly coaching and playing sessions, Carnoustie Craws ensures golf in Carnoustie will continue for years to come.

Jim Davis has lived the past many years in Grand Rapids, Michigan, with his wife, Barbara, where he worked as an editor for *The Grand Rapids Press*. With newspapers everywhere downsizing, in 2010, Davis accepted a by-out offer and later became the journal editor and executive director for the Society of Hickory Golfers. In 2013, he became the editor of *The Bulletin* of the Golf Collectors Society. In 2018, the Society changed its name to the Golf Heritage Society and *The Bulletin* became *The Golf*. He co-edited and designed Ralph Livingston III's *Thomas Stewart Jr, Golf Cleek and Iron Maker* (2010). In 2013, he edited *Great Golf Collections of the World*, for authors Richard McDonough and Pete Georgiady. In 2021, he published *The Fickle Niblick*, a modest anthology of his own articles, stories and columns. He continues his work with journals for the two societies and enjoys playing in a variety of hickory golf events throughout the country and abroad, this despite an enormous body of proof that, for him, golf is better read and written about than played.

Billy Dettlaff, MPGA. The Dettlaff family's history in the game of golf has been established over the past 115 years. Billy is a PGA Master Professional with a 50-year career in the game following in his father's footsteps. In retirement, after 22-years with the PGA Tour, he turned to researching, writing and speaking on golf history. He has authored four books on the game. In January 2019, he and his wife Geraldine established the first American Golf Memories Project – the Pete Dye Chapter at TPC Sawgrass in Ponte Vedra Beach, Florida. It was inspired by the great work being done by Lorraine Young and the Carnoustie Golf Memories Project along with the encouragement of Dr Michael Ego. The Dettlaffs have a stepdaughter and son who are PGA professionals.

Steve Finan is a journalist of more than 40 years' standing, having worked for various national and regional titles. He is the author of 12 books on Scottish football nostalgia, and recently published *Golf In Scotland In The Black & White Era*, which takes a meandering journey through Scotland's national game, illustrated by hundreds of never-before-seen images that have lain in newspaper and magazine archives for decades. He lives in Carnoustie and is married with two grown children. He was raised in a family of keen amateur golfers, but freely admits to being ridiculously bad at the game himself!

Rona Fitzgerald was born in Dublin and now lives in Glasgow. She is a member of the Federation of Writers (Scotland). She writes poetry, stories and creative non-fiction, highlights of which include *The Stinging Fly*, *Oxford Poetry*, the *Blue Nib Magazine*. Her recent work appears in *Dreich Number 8*, *Season 2 Littoral Magazine The Brown Envelope Book*, *The Arbroath Anthology*, *Marble Broadsheet*, *Fixator Press*, *Dreich Number 3*, *Season 4* and *A Fish Rots From The Head*.

Hannah Fleming is the Learning & Access Curator at the R&A World Golf Museum. Growing up in the East Neuk of Fife, she had an awareness of golf, but her knowledge was limited. She has worked at R&A World Golf Museum since graduating from the University of St Andrews in 2005. During her time at the museum, she has worked in visitor services, curatorial (having completed a Museum and Galleries Studies postgrad diploma in 2016) and is today responsible for leading the museum's learning programmes. Her appreciation for the subject has grown through speaking to visitors and those passionate about the sport and its heritage. Creating a space for people to feel connected to the museum's collections and share their stories is her main priority. Projects such as Golf Memories has enabled her to broaden her skills and appreciate the power golf has on the lives of the museum's visitors.

Debbie Foley PGA has been working in the golf industry since 1989 and has been a member of the PGA of America since 1998, earning PGA certified professional status in 2007. She worked for the PGA Tour's TPC Network for ten years before joining the staff at the PGA of America's headquarters in 1999. Her current position with the PGA education department is PGA senior faculty member, which includes developing and delivering curriculum to support PGA associates, students and PGA members as they continue their education to succeed in the golf industry. After 34 years in Florida, she has recently moved to Frisco, Texas, as the PGA of America finalises plans to open the new home of the PGA.

Susan Grant is a former teacher. After she retired, she kept fit by learning to play golf and exercised her mind writing poetry. Her contribution to this book marries the two hobbies although she has had more success with writing than with golf.

Yvonne Gray is a writer and musician whose work has been published widely in magazines and anthologies. Her publications include *Swappan the Mallimacks* (2006), *In the Hanging Valley* (2008) and *Hours* (2011). *Reflections* (2012), a collaboration with artist John Cumming, was shortlisted for the Callum MacDonald Memorial Award in 2013. She co-wrote the libretto for Sally Lamb McCune's opera 'We Wear the Sea Like a Coat' premiered by Opera Ithaca this year.

Ross Kilvington is a freelance writer whose work has been featured in acclaimed publications *Nutmeg*, *North Section* and *Gentleman Ultra*, and in many others. He is currently writing a book on the inside story of the 1998 FIFA World Cup. He is a keen golfer in his spare time, although his quest to break 80 will need to be put on hold due to having two daughters under the age of four.

Andy Jackson is author of three collections of poetry, most recently *The Saints Are Coming* (2020) and editor of a dozen anthologies, including *Scotia Extremis* (2019), *Whaleback City* (2013) and *Split Screen/Double Bill* (2012/2014). He also co-edits *Poetry Scotland* magazine.

Euan Kerr is the long-time editor of *The Beano*, the UK's favourite children's comic, and even longer time golfer on Carnoustie Links.

Hugh MacDonald is a freelance journalist who was once chief sub-editor, literary editor and chief sports editor of *The Herald*. He now writes for the *Daily Mail* and broadcasts for BBC and plz soccer. His only relationship with decent golf has been to watch it.

Ann MacLaren is the author of *Handle With Care & Other Stories*. She also writes poetry, drama and memoir and is working on her first novel. She has a PhD in Spanish and Portuguese Drama Translation.

Colin MacLean started playing golf age ten. He played at the 18-hole Caird Park, Dundee, with his dad and a bag of four second-hand clubs for a couple of years and then cycled with his clubs on his back to the 9-hole Caird Park course until he was 14. The family moved to Forfar, and he joined Forfar Golf Club as a junior paying £1 a year. In 1967, he and his mathematics teacher won the pupil-teacher match, but since they were allocating handicaps and counting scores no-one believed them. After a gap of 15 years, he moved to live near Carnoustie and played there for ten years. Moving to Edinburgh in 1996, he played the six municipal courses on an occasional basis until he retired. He now plays at least once a week with the Edinburgh U3A, playing off a WHS handicap of around 18.

Roy Mackenzie is Hebridean born. A resident of Wick, he is today a retiree, charity volunteer, local historian and golfer.

Catriona Matthew is a Scottish golfer who has had an extremely successful career across the globe. She was the first Scottish winner of the AIG Women's British Open, at Royal Lytham & St Annes Golf Club in 2009, and won a further three LPGA Tour events and five Ladies European Tour events, including the Scottish Open twice. Her 30-year career has seen her represent Europe in the Solheim Cup nine times. She also captained the victorious European Solheim Cup team in 2019 and 2021 and was awarded an MBE in 2010 and an OBE in 2020, both in recognition of her services to golf.

Richard McBrearty has worked for the Scottish Football Museum for the past 23 years and has held the post of Curator since 2004. He has been involved with the Football Memories Scotland project since the inception of the pilot programme in 2009 and took on the role of Project Director in 2018. From 2015 to 2020, he sat on the Sports Heritage Scotland steering group which helped to coordinate the reminiscence programmes for football, golf, rugby, shinty, cricket and speedway. He presently sits on the steering group for Memories Scotland, an exciting new development which will see the sports reminiscence projects join with library groups across Scotland who will support reminiscence activity using local and social history collections.

George McGregor is a former R&A Captain, five-time Walker Cup player who has represented Scotland in home internationals (1969-87), played in seven European Team Championships and captained the Scotland international team (1999-2000). Among his accolades are winning the Lytham Trophy in 1975, being named Scottish Amateur Stroke Play champion in 1982 and being runner-up in the Scottish Amateur Championship in 1982. He is married to Christine and has two daughters, Fiona and Morag. He has been a member of Glencorse Golf Club since 1953 and joined The R&A in 1995. During his time at the R&A, he has served on various committees and was appointed Captain for 2015. He was awarded an OBE for services to amateur golf in 1996.

Keith McIntosh was born, and has always lived, in Ayrshire. He has worked in the NHS for 28 years and is a married father of three boys, a graduate of the University of Glasgow and The Open University. He has been playing golf since he was 15. His contribution to Mind the Links is his first published work.

Diane McKee writes fiction and poetry. Her work has appeared in a Scottish Writers' Centre chapbook, many Dreich publications, *Writers' Forum* magazine and was shortlisted in the Glasgow Women's Library Bold Types competition. She is a member of Strathkelvin Writers' Group. After a long hiatus she has recently joined a golf club!

Julie McNeill is the Makar for St Mirren Football Club and Poet in Chief for The Hampden Collection. She is the author of *Mission Dyslexia*, a non-fiction book for children with dyslexia. Her debut poetry collection *Ragged Rainbows* was published in November 2021. Her work has appeared in print and online in publications such as *The Scotsman, Nutmeg, Philosophy Now*, BBC Scotland and *Punk Noir*. She has read at Wigtown book festival, Celtic Connections, Scottish Poetry Library, StAnza, Paisley Book Festival and Aye Write this year.

Bernie Mortimer hails from Carnoustie where he was born the son of a greenkeeper. He is a single-figure golfer who has played at Carnoustie and Arbroath, where he now resides. A well-respected caddie, he is a great advocate of the game.

Dr Andrew Murray is a General Practitioner, who worked as the Scottish Government's 1st Physical Activity Champion. He has a PhD from the University of Edinburgh 'Assessing golf and health, and investigating how the evidence can impact policy and practice' (2020). He is Medical Advisor to The R&A and the European Tour Group.

Donald S Murray is from Ness, Isle of Lewis. He won the 2021 Callum Macdonald Memorial Award for his pamphlet *Achanalt*, which was illustrated by the magnificently talented Hugh Bryden. Some of the poems from this collection were selected as among the best poems of that year by the Scottish Poetry Library.

Jim Nugent is the founder and publisher of *Global Golf Post*, the leading golf news brand in the game. He has served on the board of the American Junior Golf Association for 30 years, and he is a member of the board of the ANNIKA Foundation.

John Quinn is an ex-teacher, writer and performer from Dundee. His poetry in Scots and English has appeared in *Northwords Now*,

Southlight, Poetry Scotland, and *Lallans*. He is author of a novel, *The Eyes of Grace O'Malley,* and a play 'O Halflins an Hecklers an Weavers an Weemin', which had successful runs at Verdant Works, Dundee, and the Hamish Matters Festival, Perthshire, in 2019. He wrote lyrics for 'More Than Seven Wonders' an album of songs about Dundee released in 2021 as a fundraiser for a children's charity.

Larissa Reid grew up in St Andrews, and as such was 'steeped' in golf from a young age. She is a freelance science writer by trade and has written poetry and prose regularly since 2016. Notable publications include *Northwords Now, Silk & Smoke, Black Bough Poetry Anthologies, The Darg* **and** *Beyond the Swelkie.* She had a poem shortlisted for the Janet Coats Memorial Prize in 2020. She is intrigued by visible and invisible boundary lines in landscapes – geological faultlines, myth and reality, edge-lines of land and sea. Based on Scotland's east coast, she balances her writing life with bringing up her daughters. She is a founder member of the Edinburgh-based writing group, Twisted::Colon.

Peter Roy is a middle-aged man who believes in bladed irons, links golf and 400-yard par fours. He desperately hopes to one day play a round with Sandy Lyle. He lives in Edinburgh with his wife, two sons and their dog, Fidra.

Patricia Sawers is the Lord Lieutenant of Angus and as such is the representative of the Crown in Angus. She was Chair of the Carnoustie Golf Links Management Committee between 2014 and 2020, and during that period served as the first female Chair of the Championship Committee at a host Open venue.

Les Schupak is chairman of the editorial board and a columnist of *Met Golfer,* the official publication of the Metropolitan Golf Association, of which he is a past president. He serves as a regional affairs committee member for the United States Golf Association. Formerly a governor of the Arizona Golf Association, he is currently a foundation member of the Florida State Golf Association and was a director of The First Tee of Metropolitan New York. He is a former officer and director of the Metropolitan Golf Writers Association, a current member of the Golf Writers Association of America and has authored two books on behalf of PGA professionals.

Finola Scott's poems are scattered on the wind, on posters, tapestries and in *Gutter, New Writing Scotland* and *Lighthouse*. Her published work includes the pamphlet *Much left unsaid, Count the ways* and *Modern Makars: Yin*. Her poems are posted on Facebook at Finola Scott Poems.

Leela Soma was born in Madras, India, and now lives in Glasgow. After working as a Principal Teacher of Modern Studies, she has turned to writing. Her poems and short stories have been published in several anthologies and publications, including *The Scotsman, The Blue Nib, The Grind, New Voices, Glasgow Review of Books* and *Gutter* magazine. Her two poetry collections, *From Madras to Milngavie* and *Tartan and Turmeric*, and her latest, the pamphlet *Chintz,* were well received. She has been shortlisted for the erbacce-prize for Poetry and The Pushcart Prize, both in 2020. She is the founder of The Kavya Prize for writers of colour in Scotland. She serves on the East Dunbartonshire Arts and Culture Committee, is a Board member of Scottish Pen and is the chair of Bearsden Writers Group. Her work reflects her dual heritage of India and Scotland.

Sheila Templeton writes in Scots and English. She has been Makar of the Federation of Writers Scotland and was nominated in 2020 for a Scots Writer of the Year Award. Her poetry has won top prizes in the James McCash Scots Poetry Competition, the McLellan Poetry Prize and the Neil Gunn Writing Competition (Poetry Section). She recently won the McCash Competition with her poem 'This morn'. Her latest full collections are *Gaitherin* and *Clyack*.

Jennie Turnbull is a poet and musician from Crieff in Perthshire. She writes poems in the gaps between music lessons and has been published in *Poetry Scotland* and in a *Coin-Operated Press* zine. Her work was published in *Journeys* and *Nourish,* anthologies produced during Book Week Scotland by the Scottish Book Trust. Her limited-edition lockdown pamphlet, *Nothing Happened Here*, came out in 2020.

Lee Vannet is PGA Professional at Newmachar Golf Club, born and bred in Carnoustie

Bobby Weed has designed new golf courses and comprehensive renovations spanning from the 'golden age' of design to the 'modern era'. His work features a balance of visual appeal, sustainability and playability, all informed by an environmentally sensitive aesthetic and an exceptional hands-on approach. His professional career began in the 1970s with an extended apprenticeship under Pete Dye, which sparked a 40-year friendship. He is a long-time member of the American Society of Golf Course Architects, the Golf Course Superintendents Association of America, the Florida Turfgrass Association and is a former Certified Golf Course Superintendent.

Stephen Watt is Dumbarton FC's poet-in-residence and *Nutmeg* magazine poetry editor. He has five published collections of poetry, edited two punk poetry collections on behalf of the Joe Strummer Foundation and Buzzcocks, and won this year's inaugural Liverpool Poetry Prize open competition.

Michael Wells was born in Dundee and attended school in St Andrews. Starting his golf career with The R&A at the Carnoustie Open in 1999, he worked there for more than 18 years, latterly as Director of Championship Staging before taking up the role as the first Chief Executive of Carnoustie Golf Links in 2017. He now lives locally to Carnoustie and has three children. A Dundee United supporter, you may find him at Tannadice more than the golf course!

Michael White spent his career in education, where he taught the whole age range from 4 to 85, after which he moved into the charity sector, firstly with Abbeyfield Scotland and then Alzheimer Scotland. In 2004, he set up Football Memories which was adopted as a national project in 2009. He has developed other sports-based reminiscence projects, notably in rugby, cricket, golf, shinty and speedway. In 2016, he established a new charity, Screen Memories, using similar techniques to help those living with dementia and other memory problems, as well as those who are lonely and socially isolated. This has led to a linked project based on the pop music of the 50s, 60s and 70s. Since the pandemic he has developed online versions of the reminiscence projects and has helped establish similar projects in The Netherlands, Brazil and the USA.

Trevor Williamson has been involved in golf for over 60 years and sees golf as a vocation. His proudest golfing moment was when he was asked to be an ambassador for Carnoustie Golf Links.

OTHER TITLES BY
TIPPERMUIR BOOKS

Tippermuir Books Ltd is an independent publishing company based in Perth, Scotland.

PUBLISHING HISTORY

Spanish Thermopylae (2009)

Battleground Perthshire (2009)

Perth: Street by Street (2012)

Born in Perthshire (2012)

In Spain with Orwell (2013)

Trust (2014)

Perth: As Others Saw Us (2014)

Love All (2015)

A Chocolate Soldier (2016)

The Early Photographers of Perthshire (2016)

Taking Detective Novels Seriously: The Collected Crime Reviews of Dorothy L Sayers (2017)

Walking with Ghosts (2017)

No Fair City: Dark Tales from Perth's Past (2017)

The Tale o the Wee Mowdie that wantit tae ken wha keeched on his heid (2017)

Hunters: Wee Stories from the Crescent: A Reminiscence of Perth's Hunter Crescent (2017)

A Little Book of Carol's (2018)

Flipstones (2018)

Perth: Scott's Fair City: The Fair Maid of Perth & Sir Walter Scott – A Celebration & Guided Tour (2018)

God, Hitler, and Lord Peter Wimsey: Selected Essays, Speeches and Articles by Dorothy L Sayers (2019)

Perth & Kinross: A Pocket Miscellany: A Companion for Visitors and Residents (2019)

The Piper of Tobruk: Pipe Major Robert Roy, MBE, DCM (2019)

The 'Gig Docter o Athole': Dr William Irvine & The Irvine Memorial Hospital (2019)

Afore the Highlands: The Jacobites in Perth, 1715-16 (2019)

'Where Sky and Summit Meet': Flight Over Perthshire – A History: Tales of Pilots, Airfields, Aeronautical Feats, & War (2019)

Diverted Traffic (2020)

Authentic Democracy: An Ethical Justification of Anarchism (2020)

'If Rivers Could Sing': A Scottish River Wildlife Journey. A Year in the Life of the River Devon as it flows through the Counties of Perthshire, Kinross-shire & Clackmannanshire (2020)

A Squatter o Bairnrhymes (2020)

In a Sma Room Songbook: From the Poems by William Soutar (2020)

The Nicht Afore Christmas: the much-loved yuletide tale in Scots (2020)

Ice Cold Blood (2021)

The Perth Riverside Nursery & Beyond: A Spirit of Enterprise and Improvement (2021)

Fatal Duty: The Scottish Police Force to 1952: Cop Killers, Killer Cops & More (2021)

The Shanter Legacy: The Search for the Grey Mare's Tail (2021)

'Dying to Live': The Story of Grant McIntyre: The Remarkable True Story of Scotland's Sickest Survivor of Covid-19 (2021)

The Black Watch and the Great War (2021)

Beyond the Swelkie: A Collection of Poems & Writings to Mark the Centenary of George Mackay Brown (2021)

Sweet F.A. (Tim Barrow, Paul Beeson and Bruce Strachan, 2022)

A War of Two Halves (Tim Barrow, Paul Beeson and Bruce Strachan, 2022)

A Scottish Wildlife Odyssey (Keith Broomfield, 2022)

In the Shadow of Piper Alpha (Ian Maloney, 2022)

FORTHCOMING

William Soutar: Collected Poetry, Volume I (Published Work) (Kirsteen McCue, Philippa Osmond-Williams and Paul S Philippou (editors), 2022)

William Soutar: Collected Poetry, Volume II (Published Work) (Kirsteen McCue, Philippa Osmond-Williams and Paul S Philippou (editors), 2022)

William Soutar: Collected Poetry, Volume III (Unpublished Work) (Kirsteen McCue, Philippa Osmond-Williams and Paul S Philippou (editors), 2023)

Perthshire 101: A Poetic Gazetteer of the Big County (Andy Jackson (editor), 2022)

The Whole Damn Town (Hannah Ballantyne, 2022)

Fat Girl, Best Friend (Susan Grant, 2022)

Balkan Rhapsody (Maria Kassimova-Moisset, translated by Iliyana Nedkova Byrne, 2022)

Perth City Activity Book: Exploring the Past and Present (Felicity Graham, 2022)

Berries Fae Banes: An Owersettin in Scots o the Poems bi Pino Mereu scrievit in Tribute tae Hamish Henderson
(Jim Mackintosh, 2022)

All Tippermuir Books titles are available from bookshops and online booksellers. They can also be purchased directly (with free postage & packing (UK only) – minimum charges for overseas delivery) from www.tippermuirbooks.co.uk.

Tippermuir Books Ltd can be contacted at
mail@tippermuirbooks.co.uk

TIPPERMUIR
· BOOKS LIMITED ·

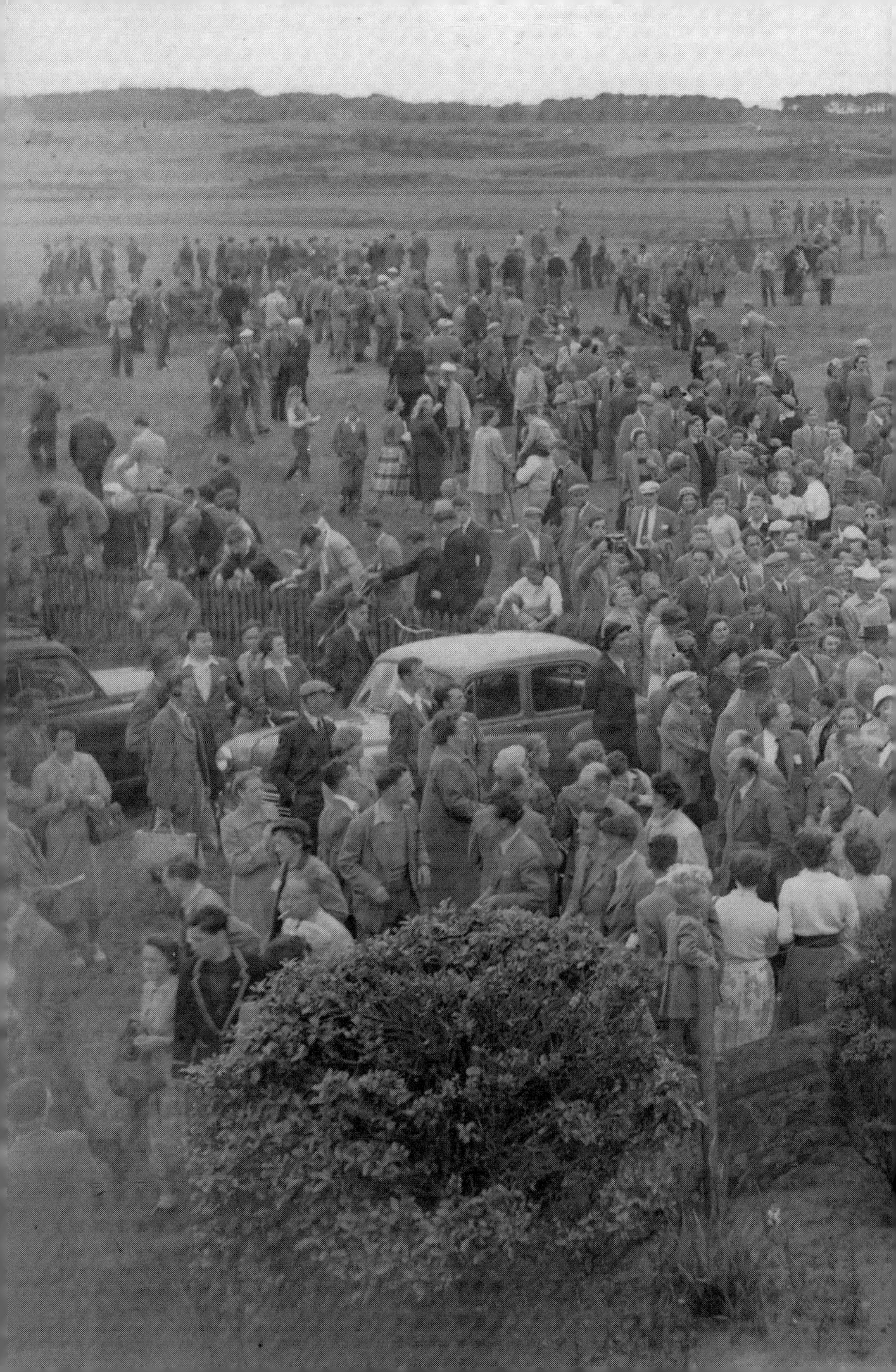

A scene at The Open, Carnoustie 1953

YOUR MEMORIES

We hope you have enjoyed the book and its wonderful weave of the personal, the precious, the ordinary and the extraordinary. One of the aims of the book is to trigger reminiscence and to encourage the recollection of treasured memories so we have provided space for you to write your own or of those dear to you or to collect a few autographs but importantly to 'Mind the Links' that bond us all.

YOUR MEMORIES

YOUR MEMORIES

YOUR MEMORIES

YOUR MEMORIES